André Téchiné

Manchester University Press

DIANA HOLMES and ROBERT INGRAM *series editors*
DUDLEY ANDREW *series consultant*

Jean-Jacques Beineix PHIL POWRIE

Luc Besson SUSAN HAYWARD

Bertrand Blier SUE HARRIS

Robert Bresson KEITH READER

Leos Carax GARIN DOWD AND FERGUS DALEY

Claude Chabrol GUY AUSTIN

Henri-Georges Clouzot CHRISTOPHER LLOYD

Jean Cocteau JAMES WILLIAMS

Claire Denis MARTINE BEUGNET

Marguerite Duras RENATE GÜNTHER

Georges Franju KATE INCE

Jean-Luc Godard DOUGLAS MORREY

Mathieu Kassovitz WILL HIGBEE

Diane Kurys CARRIE TARR

Patrice Leconte LISA DOWNING

Louis Malle HUGO FREY

Georges Méliès ELIZABETH EZRA

Maurice Pialat MARJA WAREHIME

Alain Resnais EMMA WILSON

Jean Renoir MARTIN O'SHAUGHNESSY

Eric Rohmer DEREK SCHILLING

Coline Serreau BRIGITTE ROLLET

François Truffaut DIANA HOLMES AND ROBERT INGRAM

Agnès Varda ALISON SMITH

FRENCH FILM DIRECTORS

André Téchiné

BILL MARSHALL

Manchester University Press
MANCHESTER AND NEW YORK

distributed exclusively in the USA by Palgrave

Published by Manchester University Press
Oxford Road, Manchester M13 9NR, UK
and Room 400, 175 Fifth Avenue, New York, NY 10010, USA
www.manchesteruniversitypress.co.uk

Distributed exclusively in the USA by
Palgrave, 175 Fifth Avenue, New York, NY 10010, USA

Distributed exclusively in Canada by
UBC Press, University of British Columbia, 2029 West Mall, Vancouver, BC, Canada V6T 1Z2

British Library Cataloguing-in-Publication Data
A catalogue record for this book is available from the British Library

Library of Congress Cataloging-in-Publication Data applied for

ISBN 978 0 7190 5831 8 *hardback*

First published 2007

16 15 14 13 12 11 10 09 08 07   10 9 8 7 6 5 4 3 2 1

Typeset in Scala with Meta display
by Koinonia, Manchester
Printed in Great Britain
by Biddles Ltd, King's Lynn

In memory of Jill Forbes (1947–2001)

Contents

List of figures

Stills 1–4 courtesy of the Ronald Grant Archive

Series editors' foreword

To an anglophone audience, the combination of the words 'French' and 'cinema' evokes a particular kind of film: elegant and wordy, sexy but serious – an image as dependent on national stereotypes as is that of the crudely commercial Hollywood blockbuster, which is not to say that either image is without foundation. Over the past two decades, this generalised sense of a significant relationship between French identity and film has been explored in scholarly books and articles, and has entered the curriculum at university level and, in Britain, at A-level. The study of film as an art-form and (to a lesser extent) as industry, has become a popular and widespread element of French Studies, and French cinema has acquired an important place within Film Studies. Meanwhile, the growth in multi-screen and 'art-house' cinemas, together with the development of the video industry, has led to the greater availability of foreign-language films to an English-speaking audience. Responding to these developments, this series is designed for students and teachers seeking information and accessible but rigorous critical study of French cinema, and for the enthusiastic filmgoer who wants to know more.

The adoption of a director-based approach raises questions about auteurism. A series that categorises films not according to period or to genre (for example), but to the person who directed them, runs the risk of espousing a romantic view of film as the product of solitary inspiration. On this model, the critic's role might seem to be that of discovering continuities, revealing a necessarily coherent set of themes and motifs which correspond to the particular genius of the individual. This is not our aim: the auteur perspective on film, itself most clearly articulated in France in the early 1950s, will be interrogated in certain volumes of the series, and, throughout, the director will be treated as one highly significant element in a complex process of film production and reception which includes socio-economic and political determinants, the work of a large and highly skilled team of artists and technicians, the mechanisms of production and distribution, and the complex and multiply determined responses of spectators.

The work of some of the directors in the series is already known outside France, that of others is less so – the aim is both to provide informative and original English-language studies of established figures, and to extend the range of French directors known to anglophone students of cinema. We intend the series to contribute to the promotion of the informal and formal study of French films, and to the pleasure of those who watch them.

DIANA HOLMES
ROBERT INGRAM

Acknowledgements

Many people are to be thanked in connection with this book, for providing information, suggestions, or stimulating conversation in connection with Téchiné and his work. In particular I would like to express my gratitude to Tom Armstrong, Nick Haeffner, Sue Harris, Jean-Marc Lalanne, Gaël Morel, Olivier Nicklaus, Keith Reader, David Rodowick, Alison Smith, Mark Simpson, Damian Sutton, Rose Whyman, Emma Wilson and André Téchiné himself. Completion of this volume was made possible by support from the Arts and Humanities Research Council under the research leave scheme. I would also like to thank the Faculty of Arts at the University of Glasgow. Finally, I dedicate this volume to the memory of Jill Forbes, one of the pioneers of French Film Studies in the UK, and another Téchiné fan.

Emergence

André Téchiné's sixteen feature films to date include a range of low- and high-budget productions, some involving major stars of the French cinema, some a cast of (at least at the time) unknowns, some highly successful in terms of the box office (1.1 million domestic entries for *Ma Saison préférée/My Favourite Season* in 1993 remains the highest), some far less so. The biggest critical success was arguably *Les Roseaux sauvages/Wild Reeds* (1994), which won the César (the equivalent of the Oscar in the French film industry) for best film of its year. Arguably, these two films, and also *Les Voleurs/Thieves* (1996), count among the greatest French films of that or any other decade. Most but not all of Téchiné's films have acquired international distribution, especially since the international breakthrough film *J'embrasse pas/I Don't Kiss* of 1991. The films of the 1980s and 1990s are characterised by a novelistic, even Balzacian sense of social inclusion, the interpenetration of social discourses with characters shifting from foreground to background and vice versa within the narrative, a strong sense of time and place, and a representation of same-sex relations and ethnic minority cultures which permits a sometimes radical purchase on contemporary French cultural identities in their shifting, minor modes.

Téchiné is a particularly interesting case for auteur study, in that there is what seems to be a major break in 1981, when his films become less experimental and more mainstream, *Hôtel des Amériques* inaugurating a realist, novelistic cinema which continues to this day. Téchiné himself as well as critics contribute to this narrative of the developing auteur, and this of course raises questions about the nature of auteur criticism, the ways in which (necessary) fictions involved in constructing coherence around a name or self are constructed, to what needs they are a response, and indeed their convenience, as demonstrated by this volume and series. In addition, in the Téchiné corpus certain names involved in the production process – those of actors, scriptwriters, camera operators, composers – recur, so that the collaborative aspect of his filmmaking is one that is essential to take into account.

These issues, and the films themselves, can be understood only in context. Téchiné was born in 1943 in Valence d'Agen in the south-west of France (the Midi-Pyrénées region, department of Lot-et-Garonne) to a family who owned a small business making agricultural equipment: this autobiographical fact – including the family's Spanish ancestry – manifests itself in various ways in *Souvenirs d'en France/ French Provincial* (1975), *Ma Saison préférée* and *Alice et Martin* (1998). Valence, a small town or large village of 5,000 inhabitants, is primarily a market town for the surrounding agricultural region, but as well as belonging to *la France profonde* it is very much linked to the outside world, situated on the Canal des Deux Mers that links the Atlantic and Mediterranean, and on the Bordeaux–Toulouse railway line. In many ways Téchiné's itinerary is a classic one of upward mobility in republican France. From 1952 to 1959 he was a boarder at a Catholic school in Montauban, allowed out only on Sunday afternoons when he would go to the cinema, although he often had to return before the screening ended. From 1959 he attended a secular state *lycée*, which exposed him to a different culture, with Marxist teachers, a cine-club and a film magazine, *La Plume et l'écran*, to which he contributed. His ascension of the educational system continued when in 1963– 64 he attended preparatory classes at the Lycée Voltaire in Paris for IDHEC (the prestigious film school, the Institut des hautes études cinématographiques), but he failed the entrance exam.[1] By the mid-1960s, Téchiné's professional life in Paris was moving on three terrains: those of cinema and film criticism; theatre and general intellectual life; and the wider context of Gaullist France between the end of the Algerian war in 1962 and the events of May 1968.

Téchiné sent his first piece of film criticism to *Cahiers du cinéma* in 1964 (on François Truffaut's *La Peau douce*, published in July), and became a regular contributor, writing twenty-five reviews and articles over the next three years. In this period (from 1962–65 its director

1 Some basic biographical material on Téchiné can be found in Téchiné 2003b.

was Jacques Rivette), *Cahiers* was both continuing the 'politique des auteurs' of director-centred criticism it inaugurated a decade earlier, and dealing with the fallout from the *nouvelle vague*. In the late 1950s, critics from its pages such as Truffaut had themselves become directors and contributed to a reconfiguring of the French film industry and its critical discourses in favour of an approach centred on the director as creative force, the segmentation within the general, declining film audience of a public of *cinéphiles*, and an emphasis on the specifically cinematic in filmmaking (as opposed to non-cinematic elements such as the script or an extraneous emphasis on 'content' in the form of social comment). What emerges most fully from Téchiné's writings in this period is an overall commitment to a modernist aesthetic – he cites Joyce, Woolf and also Nathalie Sarraute's notion of *tropismes* (Téchiné 1965a) – evinced in his affection for those directors who problematised the relationship between language – cinematic or otherwise – and the real; he remains attentive to specifically cinematic concerns such as rhythm, space and decor.

While Téchiné did the jobbing rounds of general film reviewing, he also wrote certain longer pieces in which his own preferences are evident. The two great Scandinavian directors, Carl Theodor Dreyer and Ingmar Bergman, loom large. In Dreyer, Téchiné appreciates the ambiguity and openness afforded by the austere and rudimentary *mise-en-scène*, in which a dynamic of meaning, freed from mere realist 'denotation', is created. For example, elements such as the slightest *frémissement* of the face in *Gertrud* (1964) 'ouvrent des horizons, engendrent des possibles' ('open up horizons, create possibilities') including those of reverie and dream, bringing with them 'une pluralité de "fonctions imageantes" diffuse, latente' ('a diffuse, latent plurality of "imaging functions"', Téchiné 1965f).[2] (This distinction between concepts in the domains of knowledge and of art – whereby in the latter they function only to allow the imagination to emerge – is standard in Kant, and is restated by Maurice Merleau-Ponty in a 1945 lecture entitled 'Le cinéma et la nouvelle psychologie': Merleau-Ponty 1996.) In Bergman, Téchiné admires an aesthetics of abandonment in which the relationship between language and silence speaks to a fundamental metaphysical anxiety (Téchiné 1965e and 1967).[3] In the

---

2 See also: Téchiné 1965b.

3 In 2003, Téchiné returned to the journal to contribute to a section on Bergman: Téchiné 2003b.

same article in which he discusses the use of spoken language in Bergman and also Marguerite Duras, Téchiné also examines Godard's recently released *Deux ou trois choses que je sais d'elle* (1966), one of the great cinematic portraits of the Gaullist heyday, the mid-decade and the 'modernisation' of the Paris region. However, he sticks to a formal and aesthetic rather than social or political appreciation. This is not to say that Téchiné neglects the real, but that he likes a cinema which, rather than being circumscribed by the real, takes off from it, as in Elia Kazan (Téchiné 1966b) or the Frank Tashlin/Jerry Lewis comedy *The Disorderly Orderly* (1964) (Téchiné 1965d). Thus among French directors Alain Resnais comes in for particular praise, in a long review of *La Guerre est finie* (1966), because his careful historical and geographical referencing and detailed *mise-en-scène* go hand in hand with, and indeed are contradicted by, inner psychological times and spaces. This means that the journeys in his films are always to be begun again (Téchiné 1966a). Intriguingly, one of Téchiné's most positive pieces on an American film is on George Cukor's *My Fair Lady* (1964), which he places in relation to Cukor's positive portrayal of women in general as caught in a world of appearances and capable of remarkable but fragile metamorphoses, as when Judy Garland in *A Star is Born* (1954) is pushed 'à mieux être elle-même en devenant une autre' ('into better being herself by becoming another') (Téchiné 1965c).

Téchiné's first filmmaking experience emerged from a theatrical milieu. The American Center on the Boulevard Raspail in Paris had a theatre school founded by Marc'O which was devoted to experimental work, in particular with regard to the relationship between theatre and music. Close to the situationist movement, Marc'O directed a film version of his 1966 play *Les Idoles*, a devastating critique of the pop-music industry and particularly the current French obsession with *yéyé* (as mainstream French 1960s pop was known). Released in 1968,[4] it starred actors from his troupe who went on to have successful careers (Bulle Ogier, Pierre Clémenti, Jean-Pierre Kalfon, as well as Michèle Moretti, with whom Téchiné was to have a long professional relation-

4 Rereleased in 2004. Marc'O, born in 1927 as Marc-Gilbert Guillaumin, has from the 1990s to the present been artistic director of the radical theatre group Génération Chaos and their magazine *Les Périphériques vous parlent*. His other films include the avant-garde *60 Minutes de la vie intérieure d'un homme/Closed Vision*, presented at the 1954 Cannes Film Festival by Jean Cocteau.

ship). André Téchiné was assistant director on this film, which was edited by Jean Eustache. (Téchiné made an uncredited walk-on appearance in Eustache's *magnum opus* of 1972, *La Maman et la putain*.) In 1969 Téchiné was assistant director on Jacques Rivette's *L'Amour fou*, also starring Ogier, Kalfon and Moretti in a theatrical setting (a production of Racine's *Andromaque*).

Paulina s'en va (1969)

It was around this time that Téchiné conceived and began to shoot his first feature film, *Paulina s'en va*. In fact, the artisanal nature of its production, and the fact that it was initially conceived as a short, meant it was shot in two periods, over one week in 1967 and two weeks in 1969, before being presented at the Venice Film Festival in 1969 and briefly released in one cinema in Paris in 1975. This little-seen, obscure work is far and away the most hermetic of Téchiné's films. The title refers to Paulina (Bulle Ogier) literally leaving the household where she has been living with her two brothers, Nicolas (Yves Beneyton) and Olivier (Dennis Berry). Her leave-taking, conducted via chaotic and sometimes violent confrontations, takes up nearly the first twenty minutes of the film. But the title also refers to Paulina leaving behind her sanity to enter a dream-like, Alice in Wonderland world. In a café she meets a mysterious stranger who works in a nearby psychiatric clinic, into which she is inducted by a nurse (Michèle Moretti) and made to answer a questionnaire which she views on a cinema screen, the words printed on a purple background. Meanwhile, a civil conflict seems to be raging, with checkpoints, sounds of shooting and the reappearance of Nicolas in chains. He is allowed to visit Paulina at the clinic but is carted off the next day as a 'deserter', having told Paulina that Olivier has left for the forest to join a rebel group. Paulina is then 'sold' by the clinic to a brothel – said to be the only functioning institution and extant building in the town – and which is presided over by Hortense (Laura Betti, who worked extensively with Pasolini), a former opera singer, and 'le vieil oncle' ('the old uncle') (André Julien). Here Paulina is subjected to endless philosophising by the 'uncle' in a room containing a massive globe of the world, and is encouraged by Hortense to participate in a bourgeois cocktail party, which she refuses. Paulina meets up again with Nicolas in a ruined town, but is then seen looking for Hortense again, only to be driven off through the forest by a mysterious man.

A plot summary is not only difficult but also possibly misleading, as the film is not only full of irrational cuts and image–sound disjunctures which disrupt any linearity, it also establishes different levels of reality and films within the film. The whole film is framed by two brief sequences in black and white involving Paulina and Nicolas. In the first, they are walking along a country road towards the camera. At the end, they are beside a lake, with only Nicolas's legs in shot, conversing cryptically about throwing their clothes in the water, 'getting nowhere' and 'starting again'. But from the outset there is another film, a silent one save for the noise on the soundtrack of the projection apparatus. First glimpsed after the opening credits, this shows a female figure (perhaps the nurse from the clinic, as she is also played by Michèle Moretti) dressed in blue, crossing a field in which a number of bodies are covered in white shawls. Later, after a few minutes showing the Paulina–Nicolas–Olivier household, the same film returns to show this same figure kissing another woman, dressed in red. The same mode (a silent film, the sound of the projector) returns in later sequences portraying the rebels in the forest.

In many ways *Paulina s'en va* is rather derivative. The chaotic, quasi-incestuous household of the opening sequence recalls Jean-Pierre Melville's 1950 adaptation of Jean Cocteau's *Les Enfants terribles*. The relationship between female nurse and patient, along with the blurring of the boundaries of those roles, recalls Ingmar Bergman's *Persona* (1966), on which Téchiné had written for *Cahiers du cinéma*, concentrating on its use of the spoken word: 'Elle est fantasmagorique, écrasée par la profusion des sollicitations obsessionnelles' ('It is fantasmagorical, crushed by the profusion of obsessional solicitations') (Téchiné 1967). Both *Paulina s'en va* and *Persona* juxtapose inner distress with references to historical and collective crisis: Paulina is confronted with a still photo of a possibly German soldier and an old woman; from the outset Bergman inserts newsreel footage of Buddhist monks immolating themselves in Vietnam, and the famous photograph of a frightened Jewish boy in Nazi-occupied Poland. In his 1967 review, however, Téchiné emphasises, rather ahistorically, 'la préhistoire inchangée de la détresse' ('the unchanged prehistory of distress').[5]

5 We shall see in the next chapter that more can be made of Bergman, and of his influence on Téchiné, in terms of contemporary realism and social relevance.

Other influences discernible in *Paulina s'en va* are those of Jean Genet's play *Le Balcon* (1956) for its juxtaposition of a brothel, social authority and civil strife (André Julien had worked in theatre with both Genet and Beckett), as well of course as Luis Buñuel's *Belle de jour* (1967), which not only uses prostitution to satirise bourgeois society, but also features significant dream sequences of journeys in a horse and carriage into a forest. And although the experimentalism of *Paulina s'en va* distinguishes it from the emphases on immediacy of the New Wave, it does not seem so unusual when juxtaposed with the work of the 'Left Bank' director Alain Resnais, most notably *L'Année dernière à Marienbad* (1961). Whereas Resnais had already developed by the late 1960s possibly the most subtle, complex and sustained body of work in all cinema exploring the relations between time, memory and history (*Hiroshima mon amour*, 1959; *Muriel*, 1963, on the Algerian war; *La Guerre est finie*, 1966, on the Spanish Civil War), there are some elements in *Paulina s'en va* which actually anticipate some later memorable Resnais touches: the fantasmatic civil strife in the town imagined by the dying writer in *Providence* (1977); and the fairytale scenes in the forest in *La Vie est un roman* (1983). And yet, there also seem to be references to Jean-Luc Godard in the portrayal of the rebel group, reminiscent of the pastiche 'Liberation Front' seen in *Weekend* (1967).

In an interview with Alain Philippon in the late 1980s, Téchiné, while admitting he had not seen the film again (as is his wont), suggested that there existed in *Paulina s'en va* certain inchoate aspects of his subsequent filmmaking which were then further developed: the close-ups on Bulle Ogier's face and her physical but especially mental wanderings are for him the basis of his use of Catherine Deneuve in *Hôtel des Amériques* and *Le Lieu du crime/Scene of the Crime* (1986), and he sees in crude form in his first film his visual practice of creating new spaces with each shot (Philippon 1998: 118). This notion of the inchoate is useful for discussing *Paulina s'en va* outside a teleological framework, and for seeing the film as a jumble of possibilities and tendencies, some but by no means all of which are developed and transformed later in his work. The first tendency is the construction of mental landscapes in cinema, and with it the potential of establishing relationships between social and mental worlds, even if *Paulina s'en va* tips the balance massively in favour of the latter. The world between sleep and wake that is here depicted is, even obliquely, a recognisable one. Often, in fact, the action takes place in liminal spaces, between inside and outside, and where the real and the virtual become inter-changeable: in the apartment, a conversation between Paulina and Olivier begins on the balcony, the cacophony of the outside world (the street, traffic) at first drowning them out, until the camera tracks outwards as they re-enter the room; in the café, Paulina is filmed beside her reflection in a surface of polished wood, and in a double mirror shot with Hortense; at the clinic, Paulina's ground-floor room is bounded by large windows which look out onto the grounds, and the door serves as a direct conduit to the troubled world outside, into which Nicolas is carried off by soldiers. The mental world is seen to be constructed of fears, dreams, aspirations that are rooted in childhood (*Alice in Wonderland*, the *Cinderella* myth evoked at the brothel, the forest's connotations of a host of fairytales, not least those involving a brother and sister, the nurse's promise to tell her fairy stories and legends, Paulina's frequent singing of childhood songs, the little girl flying a kite), the cinema (Olivier criticises Paulina's obsession with stories from films, and she recognises the silent film projected to her at the clinic) and history. Although the latter remains an abstrac-tion, the film's constant evocation of violent conflict, and in partic-ular Paulina's memory of passing 'des armées en déroute' ('armies fleeing in disarray') cannot fail for a French audience to invoke the Second World War and the colonial conflicts which followed. (The year 1962 marked the first time France had been at peace for twenty-three years.) Violence in the body politic is seen in the film to have entered the dreaming and unconscious mind. And although the piles of books through which Paulina wades at the beginning may be randomly placed, two that are glimpsed are Lucien Romier's *Explica-tion de notre temps* (1925), a key French text of the interwar period analysing capitalist modernity, and Méchin-Benoist's *Soixante Jours qui ébranlèrent l'Occident* (1956), on the fall of France in 1940.

The crisis evoked by *Paulina s'en va*, however, is not only that the desiring fantasies of childhood and cinema are failing to deliver, but that, as Hortense points out, there is no Prince Charming, no transcendence and no narrative of which to make sense. The only hint of the source of the insurgents' actions is when Nicolas complains of a general evacuation of meaning ('il y avait une parole, un sens pour tout, ils n'ont rien laissé'/'There was a word, a meaning for everything, they have left nothing'), and Paulina's drama is that of forgetting, so that she cannot piece together her story or identity. She constantly aspires to 'leave' – the apartment, clinic, brothel – but she cannot exist in a perpetual present, because most of the film seems to be about time and the mental interpenetration of past, present and future, with the past as unknowable (a cryptic reference to the massa-cring of a whole family and its replacement by a series of others). What is left are bodies, the bodies of actors, first of all as ordinary, daily bodies in the opening sequence in the apartment – spilling milk, packing suitcases, eating baguettes, refusing to get out of bed – and then as ceremonial, theatralised bodies that constantly undergo and initiate rituals (in which the film abounds, as when Hortense mourns the dead uncle in striking staged space bathed in red light).

It is tempting to see *Paulina s'en va* as a classic first film, in the sense of being too abstract and too personal, in which the 24-year-old Téchiné, while influenced by artists and filmmakers he worships, is working through his own stories: childhood, departures, the persis-tence – nonetheless – of the past, displaced mother and father figures, authority and revolt, alternative sexual arrangements. (First works can invite allegorical readings: perhaps when Paulina at the end 'enters' the film within the film, this can be interpreted as Téchiné passing to the other side of the screen, from *cinéphile* to *cinéaste*.) Much of this constitutes the raw material of his later films. One remarkable aspect of *Paulina s'en va*, however, is the fact that its creation took place on either side of what is considered to be one of the major caesuras of modern French history, namely May 1968. The crisis challenged the Gaullist regime from two directions, those of students protesting against the centralised and hierarchical university system and beyond that the state and the capitalist system, and, in the biggest general strike in European history, the working class, large portions of which felt left behind by economic expansion and modernisation. Although the regime recovered, the political and cultural reverberations of the events lasted for decades. Cinema was directly implicated. Already in February 1968 the sacking by Culture Minister André Malraux of Henri Langlois as head of the Cinémathèque – an institution beloved and frequented, of course, by *cinéphiles* such as Téchiné – had led to massive protests in the industry against this direct state interfer-ence. In May, radical restructuring of the French film industry was discussed at an Estates General of Cinema, and the Cannes Film Festival was cancelled.

Téchiné, like many of his generation, was on the barricades in

May, along with his flatmate, the lesbian feminist Monique Wittig, who in this period wrote her first, experimental works, *L'Opoponax* (1964) and *Les Guérillères* (1969), and co-founded the Mouvement de libération des femmes (MLF, 1970) and Les Gouines rouges ('The Red Dykes', 1971). (*Paulina s'en va* shares with *Les Guérillères* at least some notion of a symbolic 'war' against oppressive regimes of signification; Téchiné dedicated his film *Les Egarés/Strayed* to Wittig on the occasion of her death, at the age of 67, in 2003.) Téchiné in 1968 was a militant in Daniel Cohn-Bendit's Mouvement du 22 mars, which had begun at Nanterre University earlier that year, and he spent a night in a police cell in Issy-les-Moulineaux for fly-posting. However, he had distanced himself from *Cahiers du cinéma*, which under the direction of Jean-Louis Comolli and Paul Narboni was for a few years after 1968 to take a radical Marxist and even Maoist line whose application to cinema and the creative process Téchiné did not share. In an interview twenty years later with Alain Philippon, he spoke of the 'short circuit' produced between the creative *élan* of the New Wave and the political urgencies and necessities of the late 1960s and early 1970s (Philippon 1988: 120).

Souvenirs d'en France (1975)

Téchiné's second feature was an attempt to overcome this dichotomy. In the meantime, he had been working in television production, including directing episodes of the ORTF (state television) historical drama *Michel l'enfant roi* in 1972, and writing the screenplay for *Aloïse*, directed by Liliane de Kermadec and released in 1975. The film is a biography of the Swiss artist Aloïse Corbaz, 1886–1964, who descends into madness; she is played in the film by the young Isabelle Huppert and by Delphine Seyrig. By the early to mid-1970s, however, the cinematic, political and intellectual context of his work had shifted. Much discussion of the formal experimentation of Téchiné's 1970s films has been concerned with setting up a confrontation (akin to that between the *nouvelle vague* and the 'cinéma de papa', but in minor mode) with the 'naturalisme à la française' supposedly dominant in the early 1970s. *Souvenirs d'en France* would thus be an antidote to Claude Sautet's *Vincent, François, Paul et les autres* (1974), which also portrays, but in so different a fashion, the world of *petites et moyennes entreprises*

(Philippon 1988: 52–3). More importantly, there is the question of audiences and visual/narrative pleasure, with which Téchiné was consciously seeking to engage following the obscure destiny of his first feature. This question of pleasure also posed itself urgently to the relations between cinema, politics and history in the early 1970s, and the engagement in *Souvenirs d'en France* with the popular genre of the family saga was an attempt to reconcile the two.

In the short term, political agendas for most of the 1970s in France took for granted the fact that what was at stake was a *changement de société*, to be brought about either by revolution (*les gauchistes*), or by the *programme commun* elaborated by socialists and communists that reworked unfinished business from the Popular Front and Liberation periods (evoked in *Souvenirs d'en France*). However, the presidential victory of Valéry Giscard d'Estaing in 1974 largely postponed the momentum for change and contributed to a depressed and polarised political climate. One of the specificities of the 1970s context, then, was that the links between history and desire, and how they might be represented cinematically, were being explored anew in the light provided by the 1960s.

Téchiné's itinerary and intellectual profile can be usefully charted in relation to that of Roland Barthes. Téchiné and Barthes had met in 1972 on the Côte d'Azur when *Paulina s'en va* was shown on the margins of the Cannes festival. Téchiné attended Barthes's seminars, and their collaboration included discussing a film biography of Proust, and of course Barthes's presence in the role of Thackeray in *Les Sœurs Brontë* (1979). They shared personal links with the south-west (where Téchiné was born and Barthes was brought up, and buried) as well as their sexual preferences. In 1968, Barthes, in association with the avant-garde literary journal *Tel Quel*, endorsed the critique of capitalism and an interest in the Communist Party, and wrote on the relation between the movement's graffiti, writing, and the need to rupture the symbolic order. Certain intellectual affinities between Barthes and Téchiné are important for the context of the 1970s and beyond. The hostility to petty-bourgeois ideology so present in Barthes's *Mythologies* (1957) lies in its claims to 'the natural' and its denial of the social and historical construction of discourses. Rhetorically, the lair of myth is often that of the binary opposition. In the context of the 1970s, the urgency of 'making strange' bourgeois ideology, while at the same time avoiding the puritanical militancy of Maoists and others (the beginnings of what we might now call a cultural politics of pleasure and desire), came together for Téchiné via Barthes. Both men were also of course indebted to Bertolt Brecht, whose role is best explained by analysing *Souvenirs d'en France*, which was co-scripted with the American Marilyn Goldin (also known for her contribution to the writing of Luc Besson's *The Big Blue* of 1988).

In the manner of Roger Martin du Gard's *Les Thibault*, or *romans-fleuve* by Georges Duhamel or Jules Romains, or John Galsworthy's *The Forsyte Saga* (the BBC television series had been shown in France in the early 1970s), *Souvenirs d'en France* is a family saga, spanning the years 1936–73, with a digression to before the First World War when Pedret, a Spanish immigrant to the south-west of France, married the baker's daughter and founded the dynasty that owned the agricultural machinery factory around which the film revolves. The film, however, largely focuses on the destinies of two women who marry into the family. Berthe (Jeanne Moreau), the local laundress, marries Hector (Michel Auclair), gets involved in the Resistance almost by inadvertence, becomes an influential Gaullist, and as manager of the factory negotiates with the unions in May 1968. Régina (Marie-France Pisier), married to Prosper (Claude Mann), is flighty and frustrated, runs off with an American soldier at the end of the war, only to return in the 1970s to bring US capital and know-how to the running of the factory.

The choice of a bourgeoisie more *petite* than *grande* is deliberate, for the target is an ideology of individualism that would legitimate the social order through the observation, for example, of upward mobility and of a 'good' *patron*. The mode of this family saga and simultaneously radical film is decidedly minor. While *la grande histoire* is recounted in the film in textbook fashion, with the litany of Popular Front, Resistance, Liberation and May 1968, it is not simply for budgetary reasons that they are figured so obliquely (for example, lateral tracking shots of Pedret and son walking past a demonstration, or the noise of the *Internationale* outside the mansion windows in 1936–37). What Téchiné is interested in are moments that express contradictions, rather than the spectacle of official history. As for *la petite histoire*, the film mainly consists of a series of often domestic tableaux, in which the gestures of everyday life are made to signify historically. (Berthe, notably, sees the two *histoires* as rigorously separate, and congratulates herself at the Liberation for having joined *la grande*.) Like cross-sections of historical moments, a scene in the film often portrays the aftermath or antecedent of a moment of personal crisis or transition.

This is the reason why the film centres on two women, for the private sphere to which women have been confined is suddenly reinvested with collective significance. An example is to be found when Berthe is deciding whether to marry Hector, against the wishes of Augustine (Orane Demazis, who played Fanny in Marcel Pagnol's Marseilles trilogy of 1931–36 and thus represents a direct link to the popular culture of that decade), her prospective mother-in-law. Here a static camera films her preparing a simple meal of plain omelette and salad while she talks encouragingly to herself. The materiality of the scene, the details of the labour and ingredients, serve not so much the narrative but the project of making visible the historical construction of events, practices, desires. Making the omelette is about power and society, a whole collective tale of production and relationships is seen to have gone into the construction of the scene, and indeed its possible outcomes (in fact she leaves without eating in order to see Hector). In some ways this is reminiscent of a scene in Dreyer's *Gertrud* when, in flashback, the heroine recounts her life with a former lover. The camera follows her in an apartment, as, alone, she 'tidies up', and several minutes are spent watching her careful domestic labour, particularly at the kitchen sink. As we have seen, Téchiné admired the way in which Dreyer could draw myriad possibilities out of a rudimentary *mise-en-scène*, and with an imperceptible flicker of expression on Gertrud's face how he here suggests a combination of boredom, routine, aspiration, choice, different destinies for Gertrud, all very much within the carefully delineated context of the life of a late nineteenth-century middle-class woman.

Téchiné adds a greater political and social dimension to this spiritual kind of filmmaking, an approach signalled by the disjunction at the end of the scene, when Berthe abandons the carefully prepared meal. It is useful to invoke here Roland Barthes's notion of the *instant prégnant* (via Diderot) or *gestus social* (via Brecht), as outlined in the 1973 essay he dedicated to Téchiné, 'Diderot, Brecht, Eisenstein' (Barthes 1982/1977). In these moments, the historicity ('le présent, le passé et l'avenir'/'the past, present and future') of the gesture can be read, a whole social situation can be deciphered, but not in the name of a final meaning or of the idea or topic the tableau is meant to be 'about'. The scene summarises the road travelled since *Paulina s'en va*, a film full of gestures but which remained empty. All objects in *Souvenirs d'en France* acquire this historicising aura, from the family piano through the bottle of Cinzano in the 1960s living room of the working-class family whose life parallels that of Berthe (her former fellow laundress Pierrette is played by Michèle Moretti), to the red typewriter used by the American business team.

Téchiné here thus engages with a 'novelising' view of the world as befits a portrait of the bourgeoisie, but at the same time he resists the pull of temporalities based on progress, development, teleology, an abstract 'human' psychology, and even to an extent on ageing (Barthes 1995). Indeed, time in the film is treated ironically, in the dead time of the ticking grandfather clock in the mansion, in the repetitions of scenes and shots across different events such as the sons' weddings and the celebration to mark Berthe's award of a Resistance medal, and in the scenes underlining the way in which Berthe has 'become' the *patron*. Brechtian distanciation is also achieved through the pervading irony of the film, in incongruities of dialogue (for example, Berthe's geometrical explanation of the way she sews letters on handkerchiefs in the midst of a mundane and condescending inspection of her work by Augustine), and of decor and costume (for example the late confrontation between Berthe and Régina, made up like characters from a Douglas Sirk melodrama – or from *Dallas* or *Dynasty* – takes place in a local café filled with rugby supporters watching a match on TV). The self-referentiality of this most theatrical of films extends, as one might predict, to a framing of events whereby the house and its iron entrance gate are likened to a spectacle, its curtain or division separating the spectator from it. But in this last shot of the film, traversed by a speeding train that recalls all the lateral panning shots that have gone before and that have suggested the cinematic apparatus, Berthe's voiceover emphasises the power of seduction of the image, as she recalls watching the house as a little girl as if she were at the cinema –indeed, the local cinema is the second centre of the film along with the family mansion. This reference to Berthe's childhood also points to the pun in the film's title between 'en France' and 'enfance', emphasising the links between individual and collective experience.

For *Souvenirs d'en France* also seeks to show the historical construction of desire, in terms of its codification in the family but especially the ways in which bourgeois life comes to be desired and that desire is reproduced. Desire is the terrain of struggle in the film rather than a straightforward and Manichean class conflict. Pedret (Aram Stephan) is a likeable, paternalistic employer, a supporter of the Radical Party in the fragile Popular Front coalition. A stylised flashback portrays the founding myth of his dynasty: a lateral tracking shot follows the young Pedret from his mother, through fireworks and 14 July celebrations, to his tryst with the baker's daughter; the end of the First World War is marked by the dynamic Pedret rejected in business by the cadaverous aristocratic mayor and vowing to create his factory. This sequence is immediately followed by Berthe's marriage, making clear that she is marrying the milieu as much as if not more than she is marrying Hector, a fact symbolised by the shot of her at her wedding party in front of Pedret's portrait (the only shot of this event). This desiring myth of the 'good father', helped on by the reference to cinematic spectacle and infancy, marks Berthe's reinscription into patriarchal succession, even if she protests that 'on ne change pas de nom comme on change de chemise' ('you don't change names like you change shirts') (Téchiné 1976a: 24). The connection made between sexual and social desire, and its Oedipal codings in the modern age, is to an extent indebted to Gilles Deleuze and Félix Guattari's *Anti-Oedipe*, published in 1972.[6]

Significantly, the most important crowd scene of the film is associated not with a historical event but with a visit to the cinema, to see George Cukor's *Camille* in 1937.[7] As Barthes had argued in *Mythologies*, Alexandre Dumas's creation, and subsequent adaptations of the Camille/Marguerite Gauthier character, the mistress who gives up her lover for the good of the family and dies of consumption, is an archetype of alienation, not only in her love outside her class but in her determination to espouse the values of the higher class through noble self-sacrifice. Were she portrayed as a 'silly woman' rather than as positive and serious, she might attain the status of Brechtian heroine whose alienation provokes social criticism in the audience (Barthes 1957/1972). This perhaps provides a clue to the portrayal of Régina in this scene. Although her peals of laughter as she exits

6 The work is quoted by Téchiné in Bonitzer, Daney and Kané 1976.

7 The camera pans across a series of posters advertising future screenings, all featuring similar images of kissing couples; in later sequences posters are glimpsed of Nazi propaganda films in the war, and of a porn movie in the 1970s.

the cinema contribute to the social incongruities the scene depicts (most of the rest of the audience leave weeping, with the proliferation of umbrellas emphasising collective turbulence as well as social differentiation, again through lateral pans), one might have expected her to have been seduced by the Hollywood film. After all, she is the Bovaryesque figure in the film who eventually does leave for the USA, has her illusions shaken but eventually transforms herself. However, in order for the romantic clichés to be both enjoyed and denounced (in that kind of 'critical enchantment' Barthes describes in *Le Plaisir du texte* of 1973), she cannot become identified with or subsumed to the Camille figure, which in any case, and despite its adaptations and adaptability, belongs to a different social and historical formation from the one explored in *Souvenirs d'en France*. For the spectator to appreciate the film's irony, Régina must be in denial about her romanticism, and, here at least, 'silly'.

From the point of view of the early twenty-first century, some of the historical specificities of *Souvenirs d'en France* are no doubt lost to audiences. For example, Berthe's mouthing of post-May Gaullist conciliatory clichés about participation and the workers' need to avoid being influenced by 'des idées générales trop abstraites' ('general ideas that are too abstract') (Téchiné 1976: 38) would not necessarily be recognised now, nor even the critique of the bourgeoisie appropriating workers' struggles (Hector on De Gaulle at the Liberation telling the French people, 'Merci et rentrez chez vous' ('Thank you and go home') (Téchine 1976: 33). In fact, Berthe's destiny, and 'success', could be corralled into contemporary orthodoxies about liberalism and individualism. What prevents this happening is not only the labour of historicisation that runs through the film, it is the ironic take on desire, 'success' – and their attendant cultural representations – that is permitted by Téchiné's imaginative use of melodrama. Identification and recognition are forever here in a dialectic with distance and strangeness. What is more, identity itself is both embraced, and relativised as performance. Here the use of Jeanne Moreau's star persona is central. The modern, sexy embodiment of New Wave femininity here, at 47, crosses social barriers through various performances – and costumes – of class and role, from working class to boss, from patronised to patroniser. In so doing, she draws on a federating, national star persona of 'Frenchness', while at the same time emphasising the labour that goes into these performances. On two occasions a forward tracking shot follows her rehearsing and questioning an impending social performance in terms of make-up and language, the first as she walks along the lane with Hector to the family mansion, the second in a car along the same lane with Prosper before meeting Régina, returned from America. Perhaps no other French female star could have combined authenticity and camp in this way.

What must be stressed is Téchiné's distinctiveness here, not only from 'bourgeois' cinema such as that of Sautet, but also from the Brechtian procedures of Jean-Luc Godard, the leading example of a post-1968 radical filmmaker. Unlike in *Tout va bien* (1972), Téchiné does not call attention to the materiality of the cinematic signifier through a making visible of the financial and other determinants of the making of the film, nor does his Brechtian distancing depend on montage.[8] Rather, his procedure is theatrical, and the connection to the melodramatic tradition allows him to engage with questions of gender much more than Godard in the 1960s and 1970s, since the latter is located in a romantic tradition which figures women as signs for heterosexual male desires and fears.[9] (The exceptions are the portrayal of the women factory workers in *Tout va bien* and his first project with Anne-Marie Miéville, *Numéro deux* of 1975, which does investigate male sexuality.) *Tout va bien* is much more approachable than many of Godard's post-1968 films. But Téchiné is particularly concerned not only to factor into his Brechtian procedure the audience's pleasure: he also has no qualms about engaging with existing popular forms. Sylvia Harvey, in her work on May 1968 and cinema, makes the same point about avoiding the essentialist argument that says the most avant-garde forms are necessarily the most politically radical: 'What is being proposed here is not the sudden creation of radically new communicative structures, but the breaking down of existing popular forms which is made possible through an understanding of the weak points of those forms, and understanding of the points of internal contradiction and tension' (Harvey 1978: 72).

---

8 Although Bruno Nuytten, Téchiné's cinematographer on this and his next three films, suggests that the idea of using Eisensteinian montage for the Popular Front scenes was abandoned for budgetary reasons: Fieschi 1977a.

9 See Laura Mulvey and Colin MacCabe's extensive discussion of Godard's portrayal of women in MacCabe 1980: 79–104.

Barocco (1976)

The link between identity and performance is precisely the problematic of *Barocco* (1976). With a bigger budget than *Souvenirs d'en France*, produced by Alain Sarde with finance from Les Films de La Boétie – which made many of Claude Chabrol's films of the period – and Sara Films, this highly stylised excursion into the romantic thriller genre, again co-written with Marilyn Goldin, is set in a northern, French-speaking city (in fact the film was shot in Amsterdam). It casts Isabelle Adjani as Laure, whose boxer boyfriend Samson (Gérard Depardieu) is bribed by rival political factions and their supporters in organised crime in turn to confess to, then refute, homosexual involvement with one of the candidates at a forthcoming election. The couple are prevented by the murder of Samson from fleeing the city with the money. His killer (also played by Depardieu), seeking Laure and the money, holes up with Laure's prostitute friend Nelly (Marie-France Pisier). Returning from helping the police, Laure confronts the killer and remodels him in Samson's image. The couple escape on a liner, evading the gangsters due to Walt (Jean-Claude Brialy), a newspaper editor who had befriended Laure, being shot by mistake.

The film refers to cinema rather than 'the real'. The terrorised city recalls Fritz Lang's *M* (1931), the murk, fog and dreams of escape Marcel Carné's *Le Quai des brumes* (1938). The northern city and the casting of Marie-France Pisier recall Alain Robbe-Grillet's *Trans-Europe Express* (1966). A railway carriage scene recalls the murder in Jean Renoir's *La Bête humaine* (1938). A dialogue is lifted from Nicholas Ray's *Johnny Guitar* (1953). Above all, Hitchcock is evoked in the relentless Bernard Herrmann-like score by Philippe Sarde, in a working-class streetscape and a hair-dyeing sequence as in *Marnie* (1964). Samson's death, a gunshot puncturing his eye and witnessed through the window of a train, recalls a scene in *The Birds* (1963), Laure's flailing arms echoing the gestures of Tippi Hedren when she is attacked. *Vertigo* (1954) is of course the referent, in a neat gender reversal, for Laure's transformation of Samson's killer. The curl in the hair of Antoinette (Hélène Surgère) recalls that of Madeleine/Carlotta (Kim Novak) in Hitchcock's film.

Barocco is still sufficiently located in 1970s paradigms to question this culture of images, whose pervasiveness is emphasised in the omnipresent television screens conveying election and other news, in the filmed last will and testament that Walt plans to show to his employees, in the mug shots and identikit pictures at the police station, and in the frequent shots of yellow, artificial light – often from moving trams – shining its beams through the mist and murk (beautifully captured by Bruno Nuytten once more). The printed media are also omnipresent, in the constant hawking of newspapers, and in the litter that circulates. The process of the commodification and circulation of information is captured in the opening sequence, when a cut from the scene of the first murder takes us to the newspaper offices filmed in a lateral pan from left to right, with discussion of the crime on the soundtrack, and then a cut to commuters all reading the same newspaper report ('Le Lieu du crime'/'The Scene of the crime') in a tram, the interior shot from right to left. Nelly's base is her 'shop window', its red light and curtains promising not only sexual gratification but the visual pleasure offered by her 'radicale', in fact almost a Hollywood song and dance number. The blackmail plot around Laure and Samson is set in motion at a photo-shoot, the paraphernalia of which is emphasised. In addition, *Barocco* disrupts the expectations of the classic Hollywood narratives it cites, most notably in the casting of the same actor as victim and killer, a move that breaks decisively with notions of individualism, including individual agency and guilt, on which a genre such as film noir depends. A society of the spectacle, in which hidden forces determine events and the commodity form has penetrated the whole of life, is a familiar enough analysis. The *cinéma du look* of the 1980s, which this film partly anticipates, happily raided past cultural forms and a world of images, but, in for example *Diva* (Jean-Jacques Beineix, 1981), this took the blank form of pastiche (even if hooked on to a romantic narrative of creation and the diva's refusal to have her voice recorded and commodified).

Barocco is uncertain in its position. Despite Téchiné's apparently Godardian ambitions, self-referentially drawing attention to the image through frames, panes, curtains, snow, all of which come between the spectator and what is seen,[10] this is not a militant film, for it is not concerned to examine the historical strata which have determined ideologically and sexually what we see on the screen (and

10 'C'est un trompe-l'œil, comme si je matérialisais la fonction de l'écran ... j'essaie de montrer que c'est "juste une image", pour citer Godard, et souvent une image "barrée", un masque' ('It's a trompe l'œil, as if I was making the function of the screen into a material thing ... I am trying to show that it is "just an image", to quote Godard, and often a "barred" image, a mask'), Fieschi 1977: 23.

this is its difference from *Souvenirs d'en France*). As far as its content is concerned, its politics are very abstract, equally dismissive of the two venal candidates on offer (the election result in the film is as finely balanced as that for the French presidency in 1974), and unable to mobilise any sense of an alternative working-class culture beyond the romance narratives the film cites. Indeed, collective, popular manifestations, notably the final celebrations and street parties, are to be seen as degraded as the rest of the culture that is depicted. *Barocco* is thus ambivalent about the status of the rampant intertextuality it lays bare, as source of joy (in its *cinéphilie* but also the denaturalising readings it invites its spectators to make) or as ideological trap (in that there is no escaping it, except possibly by fading away). This is perhaps another way of expressing the tension between an address to avant-garde or commercial cinema audiences.

This ambivalence extends to the film's treatment of romance. On the one hand, the romance narrative which Laure wishes to create with Samson's killer is an empty copy, a simulacrum, and just part of the general alienation in the film. Her decision to 'remake' Samson is prompted by her experience at the restaurant with Walt and Antoinette, not only by their discussion of the departing liner, but by a performance of a romantic song, 'On se voit se voir', by a cabaret singer (the uncredited torch singer Marie-France). The distinction between her performance and the 'reality' of the film is blurred when she sits down and mingles with the customers, and when Laure leaves with the same Philippe Sarde melody playing on the non-diegetic soundtrack. To this extent, the film is simply partaking of a standard left-wing pessimism about alienation in the mass media and popular culture. The killer's makeover, cross-cut with the funeral of the 'real' Samson, reveals however that the murder was a *crime passionnel*, prompted by jealousy and romantic despair. This suggests a more subtle reading of the film's treatment of the ambient culture, for it seems to validate an aspiration towards 'love', or a utopian yearning in the face of the contemporary dystopia. Indeed, Laure's half-hearted pronouncement, 'Je ne demanderai plus l'impossible' ('I won't ask for the impossible any more') reworks one of the more utopian slogans of May 1968 ('Soyez réalistes, demandez l'impossible'/'Be realistic, ask for the impossible'), whose sentiments seem to linger on in phantom fashion.

What way might the film offer through these impasses, even as it is forced to reflect on its own status as spectacle, as a relatively big-budget star vehicle? Unlike *Souvenirs d'en France*, its reach extends beyond a historical period or specific national space. Its 'making strange' of narrative, cinematic and social conventions extends as far as the relationship between subjectivity and modernity. The film is full of sequences that link the city, crowds, movement, and cinema. In turn, Laure's physical (she has difficulty, for example, in negotiating the crowds) and mental struggle to make sense of events is rendered cinematically, in the constant play of doubles, mirrors, windows and reflections in water. The screen, as in *Souvenirs d'en France*, is a fantas-matic site. Not only does *Barocco* portray a mental universe (it could be, for example, that the action from the time she waits for Samson in the station café is in fact a dream), it is a universe whose param-eters are determined by culture and (patriarchal) power, in short by ideology, in the sense of a set of beliefs and assumptions which seek to make reality and the social and political and status quo seem normal, natural and inevitable. It is the 'baroque' of the title that offers a way of 'making strange' this reality, and even modernity itself, as the cityscape becomes labyrinthine and mysterious rather than linear and progressive, and as 'the self' gives way to transformation, as fluid as the omnipresent water in the film. Stuck in a crowd once more, distinctively dressed entirely in yellow, Laure nearly does not make it to the ship, and she is caught momentarily in freeze-frame. She has to be an agent of identity switch one more time – the mistaken identity that kills Walt – before melting into the crowd of passengers on the ship (the interior of which is never glimpsed).

In an interview in 1977, Téchiné invokes the baroque painting, Rubens' *Exchange of Princesses* (1621–25), in which one figure is becoming the copy of the other (Frenais 1977). Téchiné in fact got the title of his film from the work by Severo Sarduy, the Cuban poet and cultural theorist exiled in Paris and close to Roland Barthes and the *Tel Quel* group. His *Barroco* (1974) was one of the first contemporary appropriations of the baroque as an alternative cultural resource to the instrumental reason of modernity and its progressive periodisa-tion, and is particularly relevant here for its discussion of the baroque city. 'Like an open weave referring to no privileged signifier which would ground it or grant it meaning' (Sarduy 1974: 61), it offers no symbolic inscription to human beings within it. Sarduy's argument is that baroque proliferation challenges common sense and amounts to a parody of the bourgeois economy, and he uses psychoanalytic terms from Jacques Lacan to describe the instability of subject positions, reminding us of the 'non-fit' between reality and the fantasmatic image that underpins it.[11]

'The baroque' in the film takes nothing away from the pessimistic final scenes, in which the illusions and myths of spectacle grind on: from shots of the passengers on the ship watching the dead Walt, illuminated by floodlights, there is a cut to Nelly making herself up in front of the triple mirror. She tells her husband Jules (played by Claude Brasseur, in perhaps another allusion to *Le Quai des brumes* in which his father Pierre's role was the instrument of the failure of escape), who is bathed in the light of the TV screen, that Laure has indeed left with 'Samson'. The baby is yet unnamed, and one shot isolates her in her cot with the television beside her, the implication being that her identity will be formed by ideology and the media. Nelly then parts the red curtains in anticipation of another client. However, the baroque does have the advantage of invoking a historical periodisation in which the clichés and assumptions of contemporary culture and identity may be questioned. This ambivalent and irresolvable tension between utopia and dystopia, seduction and alienation, is fundamental in Téchiné, for he sees it as fundamental to modern life. It was an important component of *Souvenirs d'en France*,[12] and is reworked in his later films.

Les Sœurs Brontë (1979)

Téchiné's third film of the 1970s, *Les Sœurs Brontë*, is difficult to assess, in that the 'director's cut' of three hours was amputated to just under two on release. This big-budget costume film, made for Daniel Toscan du Plantier's stable at Gaumont, cast three of the biggest French female stars of the time (Isabelle Huppert as Anne, Adjani as Emily, Pisier as Charlotte), with Pascal Greggory as Branwell. The commercial dimension of the enterprise was matched, however, by its auteurist origins: in fact, a version of the Brontës' life had been Téchiné's project for his second film after *Paulina s'en va*. *Les Sœurs*

---

11 See also Buci-Glucksmann 1984; Deleuze, *Le Pli: Leibniz et le baroque* 1988.

12 'Ce qui m'intéresse c'est de dénoncer la force d'aliénation tout en préservant le caractère séduisant' ('I'm interested in denouncing the force of alienation while at the same time preserving its seductive character'), Bonitzer *et al.* 1976: 55.

Brontë also marks the beginning of Téchiné's collaborative screen-writing work with Pascal Bonitzer from *Cahiers du cinéma*.

'Literary' costume dramas had been out of favour in French cinema since the *nouvelle vague*. As Jill Forbes pointed out, historical films in the 1970s had taken various political forms in the wake of May 1968 and the end of Gaullism, and were further influenced by Michel Foucault, and the development of new academic history and its attention to popular culture rather than great historical figures and events. Films by René Allio (*Les Camisards*, 1972; *Moi, Pierre Rivière*, 1976) and even the more mainstream Bertrand Tavernier (*Que La Fête commence*, 1975; *Le Juge et l'assassin*, 1976) – not to mention Téchiné's own *Souvenirs d'en France* – had partaken of these developments (Forbes 1992: 231). These are very different films from the lush, 'heritage' cinema of the following decade, partly inaugurated by Claude Berri's literary adaptation of Marcel Pagnol's *Jean de Florette* (1986). Among work by former New Wave directors, Eric Rohmer's *Perceval le Gallois* (1979) was highly stylised and idiosyncratic. But there was also François Truffaut's *L'Histoire d'Adèle H.* (1975), starring Isabelle Adjani as Victor Hugo's daughter, which had, like *Les Sœurs Brontë*, revisited the nineteenth century via a 'real' literary family, and with which Téchiné's film may have been unfavourably compared (Jones 1997: 69).

Téchiné's project was therefore an unusual one, seemingly out of step even with his own – then limited – corpus of films. While there have been many film adaptations of works by the Brontës, only two have dramatised the family relationships. The little-seen 1946 Warner Bros production, *Devotion*, directed by Curtis Bernhardt, starred Olivia de Havilland as Charlotte and Ida Lupino as Emily in a historically inaccurate love triangle with Paul Henreid as the Reverend Nicholls. There was also the highly respectful Yorkshire Television mini-series of 1973, *The Brontës of Haworth*, directed by Marc Miller and with a script by the prominent playwright Christopher Fry. There is no evidence that Téchiné saw either of these productions; rather, his sources were literary, most likely Elizabeth Gaskell's *The Life of Charlotte Brontë*. This most instrumental text in creating the Brontë myth was first published in Britain in 1857, in French in 1877 (a new edition and translation had been published in 1972), and is still in print in France.

Les Sœurs Brontë also belongs to an unusual corpus in French – and by extension European – sound cinema (the practice is standard, of course, in Hollywood, as we have seen), namely that of a historical or literary film set, and whose origin lies, in another country, in this case Britain. The most famous example is possibly Marcel Carné's *Drôle de drame* (1937), set in nineteenth-century London. In 1985 Jacques Rivette adapted *Wuthering Heights* for the screen (*Hurlevent*, 1985). Given that much discussion of the heritage film of the 1980s has centred on national identity (Higson 2003, Austin 1996), it is intriguing to consider such examples of 'cross-heritage' movies (a term I prefer here to 'transnational', which would indicate a truly international story with a multinational production team, such as Ridley Scott's *1492 Conquest of Paradise* of 1992). In this way, *Les Sœurs Brontë* might be usefully compared with Roman Polanski's *Tess*, made in the same year, with a German star (Nastassia Kinski). While the film was shot in English but crucially used landscapes in Normandy to portray Thomas Hardy's Dorset, *Les Sœurs Brontë* is in French, with 'authentic' settings shot in Yorkshire.

The film begins with a series of establishing shots and then an interior in which a pub customer is recounting the lives of the Brontë family. There is then a cut from this 'narrator', not seen or heard from again, to the famous family portrait by Branwell (who equally famously erased his own figure from it). Most of the film alternates between the austere interior of the family home, usually shot at night and in firelight, and the vast expanses of the surrounding landscape, with 'outings' made to Brussels, the Robinson home and London. Three connected plotlines basically emerge around this theme of inside–outside. The first is that of the family's literary activities, and the sisters' gradual emergence into a public sphere, culminating in the final scene at the opera in which the surviving family member, Charlotte, is received into London society. This strand immediately connects with the film's central preoccupations with familial relationships (Branwell becomes excluded from this success narrative, signalled at the beginning when he is disoriented by the letter from Southey arriving for Charlotte and not for him) and with sexual politics (the sisters' use of a masculine pseudonym results in astonishment at the London publishers when their true identities are revealed). The second is the sisters' doomed attempt to save Branwell from his downward spiral of depression, drink, drugs and also anorexia, marked most dramatically by their rescue of him from his bedroom during a house fire. The third is Branwell's liaison with Mrs Robinson (Hélène Surgère), the mother of the – rather obnoxious – children to which Anne and he have become tutors in a rather caricatured oppressive and patriarchal Victorian household.

The family dynamics here portrayed by Téchiné are extraordinary in many ways, not least because they are in fact alternative to the dominant Oedipal patterns that have characterised Western modernity, roughly, if we are to follow arguments by Deleuze and Guattari (1972) but also Raymond Bellour,[13] since the early nineteenth century when the film is set. The mother is dead, the father (Patrick Magee) is a ghostly, largely absent entity who simply 'passes through' (rather, it could be said, like François's father in Téchiné's autobiographical *Les Roseaux sauvages*). The crucial affective and indeed libidinal relationships are among the siblings. Branwell fails to adopt an Oedipal position: Lydia Robinson reproaches him, 'Que fait-on dans les romans? Conduisez-vous en homme, enlevez-moi' ('What do they do in novels? Behave like a man, take me away').

If anything, Branwell is the object of desire in the film, carried naked from his bed during the fire, in what is also a gender role reversal (even if the female members seeking to clear up the mess made by the brother is not). This is all because the family are located in a non-Oedipal economy, even though those trajectories of individuation, social role-playing and 'adult' sexuality are demanded by the wider society. Branwell's ultimate artistic failure lies perhaps in his disappointment at not fulfilling these demands. But rather than being inscribed in a master Oedipal narrative, the family is here the opposite: it itself is a machine for fabulation, for generating meanings and stories. Roland Barthes wrote that this short-circuiting in the film of the Law of the Father led to the creation of 'une famille sororale' ('a sororal family') (Barthes 1995a). From this point of view, Branwell's story is not an Oedipal one: his self-destruction is rather about the sisters or the siblings taken as one, a repression that returns and is exteriorised on to that family member. Despite the 'star vehicle' aspect of the film which some critics found off-putting, the characters portrayed are differentiated but they are emphatically not individualised in the manner of standard movie protagonists (as in the classic triangle of *Devotion*). There is an interchangeability across the four siblings, as when Emily puts on Branwell's coat and has a tubercular

13 See for example Bellour 1978 and 1979.

fit, which calls to mind Cathy's famous pronouncement in *Wuthering Heights*, 'I *am* Heathcliff'. This also means that a kind of Brechtian critical distance lingers on in Téchiné's cinema, in that emotional identification with protagonists is refused in favour of a foregrounded portrait of social and psychic structures.

The film's spatial relations, other than outside–inside, are structured, prosaically, by that between province and city (a yearning on Branwell's part even for Bradford, but most notably in the final London sequence). Isolation is emphasised at moments of departure and return with shots of carriages on the long, empty road leading to and from the parsonage, accompanied by the howling wind. So beyond this denotative aspect a certain abstractness develops, as the film contracts and expands horizons, and distributes bodies in time and space. The most striking way in which this is achieved is in the relationship between landscape and face, notably between the empty moors and the close-ups of the siblings. While this relationship is to some extent a dichotomy, in which the moors become the space of freedom, especially for Emily, as opposed to the enclosed domestic space, it is also one of interdependence, summarising a mental world, that of writing and artistic creation, which straddles the two. Intriguingly, Téchiné succeeds in combining an authenticating 'realist' depiction of place – interiors and locations – and at the same time takes off into this 'non-place'. The real Haworth and the mental construct 'Haworth' represent an alternative, and, because of the omnipresence of death, impossible world. Téchiné comes close to understanding the appeal of its romantic myth. The final scenes at the opera, with Charlotte very much now in society, are rather bathetic. The (cinematic) spectacle served up is undermined in various ways. Charlotte is losing her sight, but chooses not to wear the eyeglasses offered by her husband, preferring to see things 'in fog', although she politely accepts opera glasses from Thackeray, who has invited her to his box. The camera then pans across the boxes and audience, to reveal Lydia Robinson, but then there is a fade to past scenes, most notably the sea which Anne yearned for and near which she died, and voiceovers from Charlotte's siblings. There is a self-consciousness about time associated with the eternal sea, the loudly ticking clock in the household, the frequent conversations about the future, and also the flowing waters of streams on the moors, reiterated by Emily's voice from the beginning of the film when she preferred the evergreen holly – associated with friendship –to the briefly flowering wild rose – associated with love. There may be a reference in this closing sequence of the film to the opening pages of Proust's *Le Côté de Guermantes* (1920), which plays on aquatic metaphors to satirise the social hierarchies of theatre boxes, their denizens likened to sea deities emerging then disappearing on the borders of their world. In contrast, the irony at the end of *Les Sœurs Brontë* is one which flees the social setting to invoke the family's trans-individual memory in a movement that is both outward and inward, closed (the theatre) and open (the ocean).

We are thus faced with a very unusual 'heritage film'. Even when they extend beyond national boundaries and narratives, such as, I would argue, James Cameron's *Titanic* (1997), these films often set up a dominant, contemporary point of view, that seeks to make sense of the discrepancy between 'then' and 'now', usually via an intervening event such as feminism, consumerism or the 1960s, and thus to knit together an overarching interpretation: 'if only that past society were less class-ridden and gave more equal chances to women, then a modern heterosexual couple could have been formed and lasted'. There is an element of this in the Branwell–Lydia affair, and the startling but predictable 'otherness' of the Victorian family to 'modern' sensibilities. Also, Emily's choice of scandalously mascu-line garb in which to wander the moors underlines a gap between 1979 and the 1830s/1840s. However, the temporal point of view upon the Brontë family is not one of superiority (except perhaps with regard to medical progress...). In any case, more often than not in the costume drama that superiority is very fragile, as the spectator position, in 'national' texts at least, gets caught in an enunciative gap between the past as authenticating origin and the past as difference, between where 'we' have come from and an elaboration of national truths and values (what 'we' are now), a split that Homi Bhabha terms between the 'pedagogical' and the 'performative' (Bhabha 1990). *Les Sœurs Brontë* not only completely sidesteps this national problematic – the landscapes of Yorkshire are not French, and the Brontës' story does not correspond to a French national itinerary – it also avoids other totalising discourses such as those of individualism, romance or 'success'. Instead, it constructs a world alternative to those values and the modern imaginary that constructs them.

Téchiné's first four features are striking for the differences between them and the departures each represents from its predecessor. Their place in his overall output can only be assessed by comparing them to what came after. *Les Sœurs Brontë* ends what we might call the first period of Téchiné's output, in which an examination of genre and form took precedence over contemporary social realism: in Jill Forbes' terms, the 'real as fantastic' will in the next decade transmute into 'the fantastic become real' (Forbes 1992: 255).

References

Austin, G. (1996). *Contemporary French Cinema: An Introduction*. Manchester University Press.

Barthes, R. (1957). La Dame aux camélias. *Mythologies*. Paris, Seuil, 179–182; *Mythologies* (1972), selected and translated by A. Lavers. London, Jonathan Cape, 103–105.

Barthes, R. (1982). Diderot, Brecht, Eisenstein. *L'Obvie et l'obtus: Essais critiques III*. Paris, Seuil, 86–92; (1977). *Image, Music, Text*, translated by S.Heath. London, Fontana, 69–78.

Barthes, R. (1995). Ce qui est bon... . *Oeuvres complètes, tome 3 1974-1980*. Paris, Seuil, 272–273.

Barthes, R. (1995a). Il n'y a pas d'homme. *Oeuvres complètes, tome 3 1974-1980*. Paris, Seuil, 996–998.

Bellour, R. (1978). Un Jour, la castration. *L'Arc*, 71, 9–23.

Bellour, R. (1979). Alternation, Segmentation, Hypnosis. An interview with Raymond Bellour by Janet Bergstrom. *Camera Obscura*, 3–4, 71–103.

Bhabha, H.K. (1990). DissemiNation: time, narrative, and the margins of the modern nation. *Nation and Narration* (London: Routledge, 1990), 291–320.

Bonitzer, P., S. Daney and P. Kané. (1976). Entretien avec André Téchiné (*Souvenirs d'en France*). *Cahiers du cinéma*, 262–263 (January), 52–59.

Buci-Glucksmann, C. (1984). *La Raison baroque*. Paris, Galilée.

Deleuze, G.(1988). *Le Pli: Leibniz et le baroque*. Paris, Minuit.

Deleuze, G. and F.Guattari (1972). *L'Anti-Oedipe: capitalisme et schizophrénie*. Paris, Minuit (1984). *Anti-Oedipus: Capitalism and Schizophrenia*, translated by R. Hurley, M. Seem and H. Lane. London, Athlone Press.

Fieschi, J. (1977). Entretien avec André Téchiné. *Cinématographe*, 23 (January), 21–24.

Fieschi, J. (1977a). Entretien avec Bruno Nuytten. *Cinématographe*, 23 (January), 28–29.

Forbes, J. (1992). *The Cinema in France: After the New Wave*. London, BFI/Macmillan.

Frenais, J. (1977). Entretien avec André Téchiné. *Cinéma*, 217, 54–58.

Higson, A. (2003). *English Heritage, English Cinema: Costume Drama since 1980*. Oxford University Press.

Jones, K. (1997). *André Téchiné: la estrategía de la tensión*. Valladolid: Semana internacional de cine.

MacCabe, C. (1980). *Godard: Images, Sounds, Politics*. London, BFI/ Macmillan.

Harvey, S. (1978). *May '68 and Film Culture*. London, British Film Institute.

Merleau-Ponty, M. (1996). Le Cinéma et la nouvelle psychologie. *Sens et nonsens*. Paris, Gallimard, 61–75.

Philippon, A. (1988). *André Téchiné*. Paris, Cahiers du cinéma.

Sarduy, S. (1974). *Barroco*. Buenos Aires, Editorial Sudamericana.

Téchiné, A. (1965a). La perte de vue. *Cahiers du cinéma*, 163 (February), 84–85.

Téchiné, A. (1965b). La parole de la fin. *Cahiers du cinéma*, 164 (March), 72–73.

Téchiné, A. (1965c). Eliza et les fleurs. *Cahiers du cinéma*, 164 (March), 78–80.

Téchiné, A. (1965d). D'un autre ordre. *Cahiers du cinéma*, 165 (April), 71–72.

Téchiné, A. (1965e). Bergman et la trace. *Cahiers du cinéma*, 168 (July), 88–89.

Téchiné, A. (1965f). L'archaïsme nordique de Dreyer. *Cahiers du cinéma*, 170 (September), 36–37.

Téchiné, A. (1966a). La fin du voyage. *Cahiers du cinéma*, 181 (August) 24–25.

Téchiné, A. (1966b). Les miroirs silencieux. *Cahiers du cinéma*, 184 (November), 42.

Téchiné, A. (1967). De trois films d'une certaine parole. *Cahiers du cinéma*, 189 (April), 49–51.

Téchiné, A. (1976). Souvenirs d'en France. *L'Avant-scène cinéma*, 166 (February), 7–42.

Téchiné, A. (2003a). Mes dates-clés, par André Téchiné. *Libération* (20 August), 20–21.

Téchiné, A. (2003b). Bergman ou la lanterne magique des cinéastes. *Cahiers du cinéma*, 583 (October), 82–87.

2

New realisms

Hôtel des Amériques (1981)

Hôtel des Amériques opens with a shot of a moonlit beach, shoreline and promontory, the gentle waves audible on the soundtrack. The caption 'Biarritz' appears, followed by opening credits over the same shot announcing the presence of the film's two stars, Catherine Deneuve and Patrick Dewaere. The credits continue after a fade to a montage of black and white archive footage of the town, accompanied by the first presence on the soundtrack of a melancholic Philippe Sarde melody played on piano and strings which will accompany the love story at the film's centre. These shots concentrate on wide angles of the town and a sometimes turbulent sea, homing in on a crowded beach and then some individual swimmers, returning to a pounding ocean and then the same panoramic shot as at the beginning of the sequence.

However, the leftward movement of this shot is suddenly interrupted by a point-of-view shot, returning to colour, from the windscreen of a speeding car on the winding promontory road, the vehicle's engine and braking the only things audible on the soundtrack. A series of parallel edits of sound and vision link the car, as it travels through the rain-soaked town, to the footsteps of a man walking the streets; closer shots of driver and pedestrian reveal them to be the film's stars. The man steps out onto the street, the car's brakes screech, and the female driver rushes out. The man is unhurt and good-humoured, the woman distressed. A point-of-view shot has him looking at her as she returns to the car to get her papers, a medium shot frames the two of them by the car as he proposes they have a drink together. In the next shot, the camera slowly zooms in on the pair as they sit at the left and right of a table behind which a glass door looks out on to railway platforms and tracks. They exchange names, as she is keen to establish the report on the accident. Gilles leans slightly forward, and tries to make small talk and jokes, looking at Hélène to gauge reactions while she continues writing, and smokes nervously. The first time she looks up, and the first shot–reverse shot of the film, comes when he pays her a compliment on her looks that begins with an enigma: she is the seventh beautiful woman he has discovered in the town. Her reply marks a first concession to his discourse: 'Elle meurt de soif, la septième' ('The seventh is dying of thirst'). He gets up to fetch more drinks and to put on some music 'pour faire plus gaï': an Italian love ballad. The camera tracks him to the bar and jukebox. She looks out of the window, a point of view shot frames the empty platforms and seats. A medium close-up sees her popping some pills and resting her face on her hand. The camera follows Gilles back to the table, cutting from behind him to in front of him to watch his expression as he looks at Hélène, who has fallen asleep. The next cut shows establishing shots and sounds of the station at dawn, and as the waitress Jacqueline (Dominique Lavanant) begins her shift. Gilles has stayed at the table throughout the night while Hélène slept.

In many ways this opening sequence announces new departures in Téchiné's cinema. The opening shot establishes a concrete, contemporary space: this is Biarritz in the present. The montage shots show that this place has a history and geography which shape the events within it. The sea is both enticing and dangerous. The beaches and cliffs of the town attract thousands of visitors, and therefore thousands of individual stories are brought together, launched and relaunched, lives reshaped. The story of Hélène and Gilles, as intense as it is, has to be understood in relation to wider social connections and networks. The setting is also a liminal and transitory space. Land meets ocean – crucial scenes take place on the clifftops – in the far south-west of France near the Spanish frontier. Not by chance does much of this opening sequence take place in the station café, as the story of the two main – and indeed all – the film's protagonists will unfurl in relation to arrivals and departures, and especially the aspirations to other places and other lives announced by Hélène's point of view shot on to the railway tracks. (Hotel corridors and the airport will also fulfil this function.) Téchiné's take on Biarritz is thus rather different from other cinematic representations, the most notable of which is Eric Rohmer's *Le Rayon vert* (1986), which, although shot almost like a home movie, emphasised the town's sunlit beaches rather than its streets at night, and its status as destination (where the heroine at last finds true love) rather than somewhere to escape from. Téchiné establishes a rhythm of light and dark in the film which maps the progress of the love affair. Despite this realism, the universe of *Hôtel des Amériques* is mental as well as social: in that moment before the caption appears, the very first shot of land and sea is very abstract; the tunnel entered during the speeding car point of view shot connotes interiority; the town as labyrinthine recalls the expressionist city of *Barocco*; the newsreel sequences are not simply denotative, they suggest memories, both individual and collective, which the protagonists inhabit.

This opening sequence is also all about narrative, unlike in the 1970s films, in which narrative was subordinate. There is an opening peripety (of sorts: the 'accident' is not worthy of the name, and Gilles throws away the report Hélène has composed). It is chance, 'accident' that has brought together these two heterogeneous individuals, and their difference is very much bound up with their star personae. Parallel editing is as old as D.W. Griffith in its structuring of film narrative. The audience expectation of a Deneuve–Dewaere pairing (their only one, as it turned out) aroused by the pre-publicity and opening credits does not have long to wait to see them brought together in the narrative, but the question remains, how will their relationship develop? Catherine Deneuve's cool, distant beauty and acting style both embody considerable cultural capital, conveying – as in the close-ups here – maximum effect for what seems to be minimal outlay. There is already a disjunction here, in that despite her perfect cheekbones and figure she wears a rather unglamorous green mackintosh and ties her hair back (for most of the film in fact), and is obviously tormented by some previous event or circumstance: what will it take for her to 'become Deneuve', and to be sexually and socially empowered? Patrick Dewaere emerged fully into film stardom much later (although he was only four years younger) through the post-1968 *café-théâtre* movement and the breakthrough, 'radical' sex comedy *Les Valseuses* (Bertrand Blier, 1974). Dewaere's persona, developed through a series of successful films in the 1970s, embodied the young, virile, lower-class type with more than a touch of vulnerability (he committed suicide in July 1982), at home in comedy as well as thriller genres. Indeed, one of the obstacles – essential for generating narrative – between Gilles and Hélène will be that of social class: she is a professional (working as an anaesthetist at the local hospital), he is much more of a drifter, having recently returned from New York with his friend Bernard (Etienne Chicot), and getting by on work as a tourist guide. His mother (Frédérique Ruchaud) manages the small tourist hotel near the railway tracks that gives the film its name.

Audience narrative expectation is also aroused in these opening sequences in relation to genre, most notably the question, in what genre can this film be placed? The point-of-view shots in the speeding car at night seem initially to indicate a thriller genre. The encounter between Gilles and Hélène now indicates romance and melodrama, in which the narrative will be propelled by the relationship between desire and social constraint or context, or, as Steve Neale puts it, 'the process of desire itself and the various blockages to its fulfilment within an apparently "common-sense" established social order' (Neale 1981: 9).[1] This has consequences for action and the distribution of bodies in the space of the film: there will be a rhythm of joining and separation between the two protagonists across different spatial and temporal contexts. One of the film's last shots is the point of view of Gilles on the deserted café table where they first met, Hélène having left for Paris. When they eventually separate that first morning, having gone on to Hélène's studio flat but not had sex, the camera tracks the pair as Hélène strides off to work on foot, Gilles struggling to keep up. This movement in space was, for example, the standard way in which the Italian neo-realists mapped relations between individuals, witness those moments in Vittorio de Sica's *Bicycle Thieves* (1945) when the father, preoccupied by material urgencies, strides ahead of first the wife then the son. *Hôtel des Amériques* also sets up a narrative enigma, as Gilles's point of view watches Hélène turn the corner: this woman, object of desire, has a past, a secret.

Narrative is also organised in relation to identification. These opening scenes are full of point of view shots and close-ups: the emotional distance of Téchiné's previous movies seems to have gone. Promisingly, those shots, so bound up with desire, have been plurally distributed between the man and the woman, so that neither

---

1 For more on the romance genre and the narrativisation of obstacles that defer a love relation that in psychoanalytic terms is impossible, see Lapsley and Westlake (1992).

dominates. What is more, the beginnings of their relationship have suggested, in true art rather than genre movie fashion, an ambiguity, even an interchangeability. The 'accident victim' suffers less than the perpetrator; both Gilles and Hélène share a vulnerability, and are in a sense 'lost', even if they negotiate this situation through different social strategies.

It is revealed fairly early in the film that Hélène is still mourning her dead lover, an architect who died in a drowning accident a year earlier. They had been planning to renovate and live in a large house outside the town, 'La Salamandre'. The name, meaning 'salamander', the amphibian which in popular myth can live in flames, also refers to a brand of slow-burning gas heater which was widely sold in France in the late nineteenth and early twentieth centuries. Hélène invites Gilles to visit, an intimacy he initially refuses, and when they are temporarily installed there, the dialogue emphasises, ironically, how freezing cold it is. At the high point of their relationship, Hélène returns from a brief trip to her Paris solicitor as 'Deneuve', radiant, her hair loose, bereft of the green coat. But the weight of the past, the twin needs to remember and to forget the lost love, undermine the idyll: Gilles, in one of the film's most intense emotional confrontations, admonishes Hélène to go on remembering, as it is a sign that he will be remembered too.

However, as intense as this central love story is, we are far from the emotional two-handers characteristic of, say, Ingmar Bergman (of whom more in a moment: see *Persona*, 1966; *Scenes from a Marriage*, 1975; *Autumn Sonata*, 1978). The Gilles–Hélène affair is incomprehensible without its imbrication in a whole network of social relationships and determinations, and, indeed, other narratives of desire. Most notable among these is the friendship between Gilles and Bernard, an aspiring songwriter – and archetypal provincial macho – whom Gilles had met in New York and invited back to Biarritz. Bernard is officially going out with Colette (Josiane Balasko), but he leaves the town without telling her. Her gay friend and colleague at the postal sorting office, Luc (Jean-Louis Vitrac) desires Bernard and attempts to pick him up in a park at night, but is assaulted by him, as a result of which Bernard spends a short time in prison. Bernard had been pursuing Gilles's 20-year-old sister Elise (Sabine Haudepin), an alienated but grounded figure who seems to desire Hélène rather than any of the male characters, although at the end of the film she does,

ambivalently, kiss Rudel (François Perrot), the surgeon who had been
Hélène's lover and introduced her to the architect. To this plurality of
characters corresponds a plurality of spaces. These include not only
the sites of the troubled central romance narrative (Hélène's apartment, 'La Salamandre', Gilles's hotel room, shared liminal spaces
such as the station, airport, and shoreline), but also the casino and
restaurant, common rooms of the hotel, and gay cruising grounds.

Although the final scenes of the film take place, respectively, with
Hélène on the train to Paris, tearing up a photo of Gilles but unable to
bring herself to throw it out of the window, and Gilles on the station
platform at night waiting for the first train in order to follow her,
there is one climactic social scene which summarises the networks
the film has depicted. The Hôtel des Amériques has been bought by
a 'Basque who has made his fortune in Mexico', and has been done
up, 'Americanised'. Gilles's mother throws a party. The scene is introduced by a very long fade (to the point of the two images being held
simultaneously in the shot) from the countryside whizzing past the
windows of Hélène's train compartment to the hotel party, in which
Gilles, standing alone against the new painted backdrop of palm trees,
watches the whirling couples in the foreground dancing to a Strauss
waltz. The camera follows horizontally from left to right the series of
revelations and reactions of those unable to join in the festive mood:
Elise telling Gilles that Hélène has left, Colette introducing Gilles
to Luc (who ended up consoling and giving money to Bernard after
he went looking for him at the park and was assaulted by someone
who recognised him as a queer-basher), Colette in tears after learning
about Bernard's departure. In a series of edits that establish Gilles's
decision to follow Hélène and Elise's meeting with Rudel, the filming
momentarily becomes very abstract, as the seemingly endless whirling
couples are shot against a black background which then fades back to
the rather kitsch backdrop depicted earlier.

There are shades here of Max Ophüls' *La Ronde* (1950) of course
(itself an adaptation of an Arthur Schnitzler play, a writer greatly
admired by Téchiné), but in fact the scene goes to the heart of the
question of the nature of this 'new realism' in Téchiné's work.
Certainly, the more mainstream cinema represented by *Hôtel des
Amériques* draws on earlier cinema's appropriation of nineteenth-
century narrative techniques. Téchiné presents a version of this which
I would call very modern, for several reasons. He presents a post-

traditional world, full of transformation, movement and displacement, in which characters struggle to find emotional meaning, a
meaning that is no longer given or handed down by past generations,
and in which the yearned-for notion of 'home' is forever elusive. This
situation is rendered in part more urgent by an awareness of time
and death that the protagonists articulate at crucial moments. Like a
realist novelist, Téchiné maps the social, economic and even political
factors – material urgencies, spatial coordinates, structures of feeling
– which determine the protagonists' situation. Notably in *Hôtel des
Amériques*, money and its circulation are made very visible, in the tiny
gestures of paying at cafes, in the purchase of train tickets, and of
course at the casino, which manages to combine in one space the
themes of money, chance, and the circulation of people and things.
It turns out that Jacqueline the waitress has a gambling addiction.
Characters are often portrayed at their workplace. More radically,
changing constructions of gender are seen as crucial to the development and outcome of sexual relationships. Hélène as quintessential
post-traditional woman is trying to find her way, Gilles has for long
been trapped in dominant constructions of masculinity which fear
intimacy and non-cliched relationships with women, and which fail to
engage with the nature of his homosocial[2] friendship with Bernard,
one problem with which may be the need to disavow anything sexual
between them. The prison scenes underline this fact, when a shot–
reverse shot between them is filmed through a partition, and when
the camera pans up the prison wall (with Gilles ironically saying he is
now 'freer' in his relationship with Hélène) after it has followed the
two men following Bernard's release. However – and this is why his
films are to be seen as so modern – Téchiné's protagonists are never
actually determined by these determinants. They exist liminally, on
an undecidable frontier between situation and freedom, place and
somewhere else, illustrated physically – but also ambivalently, since it
represents the past – by the utopian architectural project of Hélène's
dead lover, a model of which is one of the few objects on display at
'La Salamandre'.

What is the relation of the Brechtian filmmaker of the 1970s to
the more realist and melodramatic aspect of *Hôtel des Amériques*?

2 For the term 'homosocial' see Sedgwick 1985. This defamiliarisation of heterosexuality is what makes Téchiné so different from Truffaut: see Chapter 3, pp.
   80, 85.

Some of the orthodoxies of *Screen* theory which dominated debate in film studies in Britain and America in the late 1970s and the 1980s tended to demonise the realist tradition. Colin MacCabe's notion of the 'classical realist text' that emerged out of the nineteenth-century novel saw it as dominated by a 'truth of the text', exacerbated by the intervening omniscient narrator, and unable to articulate social and therefore political contradictions (MacCabe 1981). However, as Sylvia Harvey (Harvey 1978) and Terry Lovell (Lovell 1980) pointed out at the time, it by no means follows that a Brechtian approach to filmmaking has to be avant-garde in form and eschew realism. Indeed, one of the key rediscoveries of this period was the work of the German émigré director Douglas Sirk, who in 1950s Hollywood brought a Brechtian approach to seemingly mainstream melodramatic scripts such as *All That Heaven Allows* (1955) and *Written on the Wind* (1956), which through irony and excess pointed out the social contradictions of Eisenhower's America. *Hôtel des Amériques* takes up many aspects of the romance genre and even soap opera. Its sequence most characterised by melodramatic excess is when Gilles, partly under the influence of alcohol, has a breakdown and throws himself into the sea at night on the pretext that if he died he would mean more to Hélène. Accompanied by a dramatic change on the music soundtrack, with sweeping strings replacing the repeated love theme, she pulls him out of the waves and they begin kissing (in a scene which is a variation on the famous coupling of Burt Lancaster and Deborah Kerr in Fred Zinneman's *From Here to Eternity*, 1953). Moreover, this Sirkian dimension to Téchiné is arguably perfectly compatible with that other strand in his filmmaking which is close to Bergman. In an analysis of *Persona*, Christopher Orr has persuasively argued that its content is supremely social rather than metaphysical:

> Although the hyperaffectivity of melodrama seems at odds with the dispassionate reflection Brecht advocated, the moments of intense emotion in *Persona*, like those in other subversive melodramas, are a response to ideological contradictions, sites of excess that implicitly defamiliarise a social order perceived as natural. (Orr 2000: 107)

Téchiné's defamiliarising cinema is also, as we have seen, profoundly plural. His 'novelising' approach at its best recalls that defence, from the left, of the nineteenth-century novel, by Mikhail Bakhtin. Bakhtin emphasised the 'polyglossia' of the novel, the portrayal of a complex society of different social and therefore ideological positions, a diversity of interpenetrating individual voices: 'A particular language in a novel is always a particular way of viewing the world, one that strives for social significance' (Bakhtin 1981: 263). For Bakhtin, 'The novel foregrounds not the technical materiality of language but the social materiality of discourse: the irreducibly plural material of social relations – of contradiction and historical becoming – is at once the irreducible material of the novel and its object of representation' (Pechey 1989: 49). I would therefore disagree with Téchiné's assessment of his secondary characters in a 1982 *Cahiers du cinéma* interview (Sainderichin and Tesson 1982), in which he sees them as caught in the 'tourbillon' ('whirlwind') of images of being in the world, whereas Gilles and Hélène try to resist. The secondary characters mark an essential continuity with the central couple's drama, not least in the defamiliarising of heterosexuality provided by Luc.

Téchiné's combination of the melodramatic mode, defamiliarisation and polyglossia marks therefore a continuity with some of his 1970s preoccupations. However, the differences from *Souvenirs d'en France* are clear. Much of this is due to a changed social and political climate. Although it would be reductive to 'read off' a direct link with the election of the socialist François Mitterrand to the Presidency in 1981, the year of the film's production, it is clear that the political climate in France had changed since the 1970s. Despite the persistence of mass unemployment, the intellectual and political *décrispation* (relaxation) of the 1980s was welcomed by many artists and intellectuals who had opposed Gaullism and Giscard. In addition, these developments raised the question of what an oppositional cinema in this new climate might consist of, indeed what meaning the term 'oppositional' now had.

As the 1980s and 1990s wore on, the absence of national or geopolitical alternatives to capitalism arguably meant, for as 'social' a filmmaker as Téchiné, a refocusing on what we might call long-term 'civilisational' rather than political questions. This meant an interest in modernity itself, the conditions in which people live this period of capitalist development. There was therefore a place for what we might call Téchiné's melodramas of modernity, or indeed, as we shall see, modernist melodramas.

In *Cahiers du cinéma* in 1982, Téchiné noted that the two main characters of *Hôtel des Amériques* began to exist only when they lost their social roles, in fact when they got scared (Sainderichin and

Tesson 1982: 37) – to which one might also add, 'woke up': a motif of sleep and awakening runs through the film. *Hôtel des Amériques* ends with Gilles having become as fragile as Hélène in the opening scene: sitting on a railway platform, moved to tears, *rehearsing* the conversation he hopes to have with her in Paris. This fascination with performance and identity is the major preoccupation of Téchiné's next feature film, *Rendez-vous* (1985).

The four-year gap between feature films is a comment on the state of Téchiné's career in the early 1980s. The combination of being well established and yet obliged to deal with the inherent instability of the production system meant that the opportunity for regular filmmaking could never be guaranteed. *Hôtel des Amériques* had been the result of Deneuve and Dewaere already being engaged for another film project, *Mexico Bar*, which for budgetary reasons was never made. Three feature film projects collapsed in the four-year period up to 1985, including an adaptation of Marie Cardinal's novel about the mother–daughter relationship, *Les Mots pour le dire* (1975, eventually filmed by José Pinheiro, 1983), and an adaptation of Pascal Bruckner's 1981 novel *Lunes de fiel*, which was to star Alain Delon. (The novel was eventually filmed in English as *Bitter Moon* by Roman Polanski in 1992.) Neither *Les Sœurs Brontë* nor *Hôtel des Amériques* had met with great box-office success. A pattern of more frequent filmmaking has occurred in Téchiné's career in the aftermath of major prizes: *Rendez-vous* won the director's prize at Cannes, and was followed by two films in two years, *Le Lieu du crime* (1986) and *Les Innocents* (1987), followed by another fallow period. The César for *Les Roseaux sauvages* consolidated Téchiné's strong position in the 1990s, and was followed in quick succession by *Les Voleurs* (1996) and *Alice et Martin* (1998), but the critical and box-office failure of the latter led to another difficult period, during which the low-budget and starless *Loin* (2000) was made, on digital video.

However, Téchiné did make two short films in the early 1980s. *La Matiouette* (1983) was made in black and white for a television series *Télévision de chambre*, produced by Jean Collet for INA (the Institut national de l'audiovisuel). Scripted by Jacques Nolot, it recounts the return home to the south-west by a gay actor based in Paris, and his encounter with his brother who continues to run the barber shop in the small town. *L'Atelier* (1984) was a film about theatre (and film) director Patrice Chéreau's actors' company at the Théâtre des

Amandiers at Nanterre outside Paris, in which the actors rehearse scenes from Dostoyevsky's *The Possessed* and Bergman's *From the Life of the Marionettes*. Téchiné situates the film in his developing interest in the 1980s in the relationship with his actors, and thus the greater intimacy inaugurated by *Hôtel des Amériques*. Precise preparation as regards position, voice and gesture, and extensive rehearsals before shooting, exist in tension in his practice with a certain suppleness when it comes to the shoot itself, including departures from the script. Téchiné's exploration in *L'Atelier* was to work with actors unaccustomed to the camera, and to emphasise the difference from the 'magnification' required in the theatre. In a later interview, Téchiné spoke of his preference for a plainer, almost unprofessional acting style ('le dénuement du jeu'),[3] in which the inner potential of the body in space is favoured over a self-conscious or exaggerated approach.

Rendez-vous (1985)

Rendez-vous contains elements from both these films. It was written – with *Cahiers* critic and filmmaker Olivier Assayas – and shot in the space of a few weeks, in a febrile atmosphere with Téchiné under great professional pressure despite the support of producer Alain Terzian. Martine Giordano's crisp editing adds to the breakneck pace of its 82 minutes. The film occupies a problematic place in his *œuvre* in terms both of its very divided critical reception[4] and what periodisation might make sense for assessing this auteur. It opens elliptically, with the view from a train arriving at the platform of the Gare d'Austerlitz in Paris, the tannoy announcing its arrival from Toulouse. The next scene introduces the central protagonist, Nina (Juliette Binoche, in her first starring role), an 18-year-old actress from the south-west hoping to make her career in Paris. The film in fact inaugurates the Binoche star persona, combining the fresh-faced *gamine* with the romantic passion associated with her later roles for Léos Carax and Louis Malle, among others (Vincendeau 2000). She meets the first of three men who are to be decisive for her development. Paulot (Wadeck Stanczak) is a shy, practical young estate agent whom she invites to see her perform her small role as a maid in a boulevard comedy. Paulot then accompanies

3 Téchiné 1996: 43. See also Philippon 1983.
4 Tom Milne called it 'empty chic' (Milne 1986).

her through the Parisian night first to her current boyfriend Fred's (Jean-Louis Vitrac) flat for a dinner that ends in a major row, then to his own home where his flatmate Quentin (Lambert Wilson) refuses to have her stay, and then to a hotel room, which he leaves when Nina complains of being used sexually by men. She then begins an intense and violent liaison with Quentin, who is an actor performing in a live sex show version of *Romeo and Juliet*. Quentin is run over and killed by a car, in what seems to be a suicide. The only other person attending his funeral is a theatre director, Scrutzler (Jean-Louis Trintignant), who eventually explains that in London he had cast Quentin as Romeo, but he had withdrawn after he survived a suicide pact with Scrutzler's daughter, with whom he had had a passionate love affair. Nina experiences visions of Quentin begging her not to take the role. Scrutzler now casts Nina as his new Juliette. Nina and Paulot make love for the first time despite an early undertaking that their relationship would be platonic. The violent and degrading coupling is followed by Paulot tearing up the tickets to *Romeo and Juliet* that she had given him, and Nina nervously preparing for her entrance in the role, Scrutzler having left declaring that his work was done.

Rendez-vous provides a very stark example of the twin elements of Téchiné's filmmaking: the evocation of real, and of virtual or mental worlds. At one level, the film continues Téchiné's engagement with melodrama. The central female protagonist deals with the attractions and dangers of heterosexual masculinity across three (four, including Fred) avatars: the father figure, and the central pair, who, unlike in, say, *Gone With The Wind*, turn out to contain elements of each other: the dependable and non-artistic Paulot (an Ashley Wilkes who eventually shows a violent side), and the Romantic, black-garbed Quentin (the Rhett Butler who turns out to be deeply scarred emotionally, and to have had one true love: his brutal encounters with Nina are punctuated by one of the few moments of tenderness in the film, as, shot from above, the couple in bed slowly change post-coital positions). To this melodrama is added an element of magic or the surreal: the three appearances of Quentin as a ghost. Here the supernatural is used to emphasise the fact that this is a film about time: the weight of memory and the inescapability of the past, and the future-oriented trajectory of Nina herself.

The title of the film can thus be read in the plural (a series of encounters – including an encounter with someone else's past

– marking Nina's trajectory) and the singular (she ultimately has a 'rendez-vous' *with herself*, having surpassed the dependency, exploitation, attachment, disappointment and apprenticeship associated with her relations with the men in the film). These encounters take place across disruptions associated with the idea of home. Nina is constantly deterritorialised, from the opening scenes on the railway through the estate agents' and the first peripatetic night with Paulot. Even when Paulot finds her a half-derelict apartment she is not safe within it, witness Quentin's irruptions, and even a particularly distasteful scene of voyeurism and near-sexual assault when she is sleeping. These deterritorialisations contribute to the film's fundamental notion of change and transformation, of 'becoming-other'.

However, questions arise here as to the meaning of the relationship with the theatre and acting, and of the nature of the process of change. A more conventional approach might be to set up an opposition between truth and falsehood around the metaphor of acting (the basis, for example, of Douglas Sirk's 1959 racial melodrama *Imitation of Life*). Indeed, Paulot echoes this very sentiment when he says to Nina, 'L'amour, c'est pas dans ton théâtre de merde, c'est dans la vie' ('Love isn't in your shitty theatre, it's in life'). This would impel a straightforward, teleological narrative of apprenticeship, whereby Nina would by the end have discovered the 'truth' about herself. However, *Rendez-vous* eschews this kind of psychological realism. Paulot has in his life tipped too far into a denial of art and representation, associating it with death: his denial of death puts a brake on his development and makes him less of a sympathetic figure in the last third of the film. (Quentin, on the other hand, is bewitched by death – and attempts to make Nina feel the same – and thus has difficulty in getting beyond the 'live' sex show to love and life.) The final scene has Nina about to play Juliette, out of frame: the future, and who Nina might be or become, is open. The very final shot of the film shows the shadow of the theatre curtain lifting over the orchestra and the backdrop, in a movement that counters the downward closing of the partition at the crematorium when Quentin's coffin is consigned to the flames. A caption quotes the line from St John's Gospel (12:22) that may refer to Quentin's sacrifice but which, because of its association with André Gide's 'coming-out' autobiography, *Si le grain ne meurt/If It Die* (1920), also speaks to the inner 'deaths' which are necessary for change and metamorphosis.

This rejection of psychological realism in *Rendez-vous* is consistent with the priority Téchiné gives, in the construction of his characters, to change, transformation and becoming:

> A partir du moment où l'on crée un personnage, il me paraît nécessaire qu'à un moment, il ne sache plus qui il est... Le personnage doit se trouver en défaut par rapport à toutes ses constructions imaginaires... Il ne doit pas être casé dans un registre psychologique sans dimension d'altérité. Cela n'aurait aucune pertinence car, dans la vie, les choses ne se passent pas ainsi. Il doit devenir étranger à lui-même et apprendre de lui-même par corrections successives. Je ne crois pas en l'apprentissage humain. Cela supposerait une forme d'adaptation humaine, ce qui me semble faux. Cependant, on peut sans cesse se corriger, sans qu'il y ait de dernier mot ou de dernière parole débouchant sur une parfaite adaptation. (Jousse and Strauss 1994: 13)[5]

This could be a description of the characters of *Hôtel des Amériques*. However, *Rendez-vous* takes the process further, and this marks its problematic status within Téchiné's *œuvre*. For the lack of psychological realism goes hand in hand with a minimising of the carefully delineated physical, geographic and social realism and plural networks of his previous feature film. Paris – often shot at night – is 'real' but fantasmatic: illuminated fountains, grey, wintry skies, Christmas shop displays and decorations to which the characters are indifferent. We learn nothing of Nina's back-story, she is a blank slate when she arrives in Paris. She is portrayed in a sexual world – another *ronde* (indeed a Schnitzler story was briefly a point of departure for Téchiné and Assayas' script) – but not a social one. Thus her 'rendez-vous' are with men, and she barely interacts with the two much more minor women characters in the film: the estate agent Gertrude and the unnamed theatre administrator (nonetheless splendid turns by Dominique Lavanant and Anne Wiazemsky respectively).

5 'From the moment a character is created, it seems to me necessary that at a certain point they no longer know who they are ... The character must find him or herself as lacking with regard to their imaginary constructions ... They must not be classified psychologically, without another dimension. That would be irrelevant, for life is not like that. They must become strangers to themselves and learn from themselves through successive corrections. I do not believe in human apprenticeship. That would assume a form of human adaptation, which seems false to me. However, we can correct ourselves endlessly, without there being a last word leading to a perfect adaptation.'

Where to place the film in Téchiné's developing output? At first sight its stylisation seems a throwback to the 1970s. Kent Jones, on the other hand, views it as a new inflection in his work, and places the elegiac, mournful *Hôtel des Amériques* closer to *Les Sœurs Brontë* (Jones 1997: 92–93). I would argue that *Rendez-vous* reminds us of the persistence in Téchiné's work of notions of doubling and phantoms, of the virtual self or selves that always co-exist with the seemingly (socially and psychologically) positioned self. This is the key – a 'becoming-other' – to the motif of acting in the film, and without it Téchiné's social realism would be a determinism. The radicalism of Téchiné's filmmaking lies in the way the 'real' is always shadowed by the 'virtual'. This means, as we shall see, that the seemingly far more conventional films of his later output are closer to what Gilles Deleuze has called the cinema of the 'time-image' rather than the 'movement-image'. In the latter, characters are unified loci of actions unfolding spatially according to chains of action and reaction, conflict and resolution. In the time-image, disparate temporal perspectives overlap and conflict without being resolvable in a 'sensory-motor situation'. Rather, we get hesitations between pasts and futures, and the possibility of belonging to different, incompatible but coexisting sets (Deleuze 1985/1988). In *Rendez-vous*, there is an affirmation of the power to affect and to be affected by, and to metamorphose. In *Hôtel des Amériques* and later films, this is intensified by the plurality of characters and the plurality of ways of being in the world.

J'embrasse pas (1991)

To illustrate this development, we can look at Téchiné's ninth feature, *J'embrasse pas* (1991), which to some extent is a remake of *Rendez-vous* or at the very least forms a kind of diptych with it (or triptych, if we include *La Matiouette*). It was filmed after a four-year gap since Téchiné's last feature, during which time a project set in Brazil had collapsed. *J'embrasse pas* was based on a story by Téchiné's collaborator Jacques Nolot, with dialogues by Téchiné, Nolot, and the writer Michel Grisolia. As Téchiné puts it in the interview on the film's DVD (Téchiné 2004), instead of a French film set in Brazil he made a kind of Brazilian film set in Paris.

Twenty-year-old Pierre (Manuel Blanc) leaves his home in a remote district of the Pyrenees to travel to Paris, where he entertains vague notions of becoming an actor. There he encounters a middle-aged nurse, Evelyne (Hélène Vincent), whom he had briefly met when working as a stretcher-bearer at Lourdes. Evelyne helps him get a job as a hospital orderly, and he begins a short-lived sexual liaison with her. His work colleague Saïd (Roschdy Zem) introduces him to an older gay couple, the cellist Dimitri (Ivan Desny), who is a kind of sexual sugar daddy to Saïd, and the intellectual television personality Romain (Philippe Noiret), who is fascinated by Pierre but who insists his interest is platonic. Pierre refuses support from Romain and Evelyne, fails dismally at his acting class, loses his job, and, broke and homeless, eventually turns to prostitution. He enjoys success in his new profession, and becomes infatuated with another prostitute, Ingrid (Emmanuelle Béart), whose dream had been to become a singer. They make love and spend an idyllic day together, but their liaison is discovered by her pimp (Christophe Bernard), who with his gang beats up and rapes Pierre, forcing Ingrid to watch. A coda shows Pierre doing anticipated military service in the paratroop regiment, and telling his shepherd brother that he intends to return to Paris as he is now ready for it. The last scene of the film has him swimming in the sea.

Nolot's *La Matiouette* featured the return of a gay actor (Patrick Fierry) from Paris to his small town in the south-west, to confront, at first anonymously, his brother (Nolot) who still runs the family barber shop. (The title is southwest slang for a character who is talked about but not seen, in this case the barber's wife.) Filmed in black and white with two cameras (a practice Téchiné adopted for his later films), it is a chamber piece reminiscent of Bergman, a two-hander with extensive use of close-ups, but, as Kent Jones points out, it uses out-of-frame sound, external shots of the countryside and of the arrival by car, and a brief interlude outside the shop to remind us of the outside world (Jones 1997: 82–83). In addition, the set design is used in detailed ways, reminiscent of the practice of *gestus* from *Souvenirs d'en France*. *J'embrasse pas* marks an opposite narrative itinerary, the familiar one of the provincial figure arriving in Paris, traversing its complex world, experiencing success or failure. It is a film about money, commerce, materiality, to the extent that *Cahiers du cinéma* called it 'un film qu'on pourrait dire marxiste en mineur ou en filigrane' ('a film we could call Marxist, in minor mode or implicitly') (Jousse 1991). The model here is of course Balzac, for long held in high regard by Marxist critics for his dissection of the emerging early nineteenth-century capitalist world in the novels of the *comédie humaine*, and beyond that the tradition of the *Bildungsroman*, or novel of education. Unlike the stable communities of the traditional past, modernity requires 'an uncertain exploration of social space' (Moretti 1987: 4) through narratives of mobility, unexpected hopes, dissatisfaction, restlessness; 'youth' was a way of giving meaning to these processes. Pierre, like a Balzac hero, is, once in Paris, forced to live a novelistic life. If we compare the setting in motion of the narratives of *Hôtel des Amériques* and *J'embrasse pas*, whereas the former depends on chance, on peripety, in the first encounter of the couple, in the latter it is modernity itself which precipitates mobility and the bringing together of heterogeneous individuals. The largely wordless early-morning opening sequence at Pierre's parents' home and shop in the Pyrenees, a fully sketched background absent from *Rendez-vous*, is remarkable for its use of silence to convey emotional repression, but also the sounds of a delivery lorry and motor scooter to signal not only a contrast with this but also the fact that modernity, in the form of national institutions and distribution, has long arrived even in this bleak corner. Paris represents of course the centre of these processes. There Pierre's 'narrative of youth' 'acts to magnify the indifferent and inhuman vigour of the modern world, which it reconstructs – as if it were an autopsy – from the wounds inflicted upon the individual' (Moretti 1987: 164). Pierre's itinerary in the film is about what possibilities there are for affection in modernity, in a world of lost tradition and discredited notions of 'home', commodified sex, and competitive individualism. But in addition, Téchiné's resolutely non-formulaic and non-abstract portrait combines the social and the intimate, as Pierre's family story, and dominant constructions of masculinity, also conspire to make him reject the relations of reciprocity offered him by both Evelyne and Romain.

These processes are beautifully captured in the sequence when Serge, Pierre's other brother, visits him in Paris, on leave for the day from his military service. Coming just over halfway through the narrative, it recapitulates and relaunches certain aspects of Pierre's story. At this stage in the narrative, Pierre has burned his bridges with Evelyne and Romain, abandoned the acting class, and is back, penniless, in lodgings. The previous scene has him rehearsing in front of

the mirror – a recurring motif – the role of beggar. His brother's tap
on the window awakens him from a slumber exacerbated by a bout
of flu (we recall the train guard awakening him as he first arrives
in Paris, and the motif of sleep and wake in *Hôtel des Amériques*).
As Pierre opens the ground-floor window to greet him, the use of
cinemascope, dominant throughout this five-minute sequence, rather
than shot–reverse shot, in the exchanges between the two young men,
places them in a shared space in which they move towards or away
from each other, onlookers on the city but also dwarfed by it. The
brother briefly paces round the front courtyard of the lodging house,
inspecting it, moving behind the iron railings through which the
pair's next conversation is shot. Continued later through the bars of
the overhead metro station, these connote, rather straightforwardly,
motifs of confinement: Pierre has hit rock bottom at this stage in the
film. Wider emotional prisons are also suggested (as well as the literal
cells when he briefly gets arrested to be with Ingrid), as when they
are dismissive of Evelyne's romantic attachment to Pierre. At the very
least, the suggestion is that the young men are the bearers of grids of
meaning and boundaries, with little active purchase upon them. In
addition, ironwork is a building and decorative technology very much
associated with the (later) nineteenth century, a fact emphasised by
the shot of the Eiffel Tower from the tourist boat. So the journey and
movement through Paris, begun as the camera follows them down a
street from behind, is inaugurated by an image of stasis.

  The boat journey echoes a previous night when Pierre, homeless,
walked across a bridge, the tourist commentary from the boat below
mocking his predicament with its indifference and otherness to this
plight. The brothers pay no attention to the sights, because for Pierre
the visit is in fact a journey home to an unhappy household, and an
abusive father. The next sequence has them crossing the Seine on an
overhead metro line, shot close-up from behind as the bleak, wintry
and distant cityscape (cinematically) unfurls before them, a distant
relationship with a place of which they can be only spectators. As
they descend the iron staircase, the brother remarks on the crowds
of people, and Pierre, hungry and ill, throws up at the point when his
brother tells him to write more often to his mother.

  The sequence ends at the railway station from which Serge has to
return to his regiment. The men are shot facing a café counter, where
Pierre eats voraciously but the brother remarks on the poor quality of

the ham as compared to home (the opening sequence had the father placing a beautiful ham in the shop display cabinet). Conversation about their unmarried shepherd brother Guy leads to an outburst from Pierre against marriage and his father, declaring his desire to bring his mother to Paris for a few days, and that soon he will have 'lots of money'. The camera follows his brother as he sprints to his train, to be swallowed up by other soldiers in uniform, a role and identity of sorts, that anticipates the film's final sequence. This is followed by an overhead shot of Pierre in the middle of the frame, surrounded by the anonymous station crowd, accompanied by the melancholy motif of Philippe Sarde's score. The camera follows him as he walks forward and stops, then an editing cut places him at a greater distance, as he walks forward, momentarily more isolated in the frame, then forward again out of frame, until the station floor is briefly almost empty, before being filled by the coming and going of anonymous individuals. (Here the use of cinemascope, as for example in the Spanish sequence in which Pierre, at a loss, wanders alone across the frame, emphasises open, empty spaces in which Pierre is failing to make connections.)[6] The next shot has him returning at night to the cruising ground, composing a smiling face for the punters, rehearsing the role not now of beggar but of prostitute.

Pierre's story is thus packed with specificities which take him, and the film, beyond a mere allegory of modernity. In fact, the film also offers utopian spaces, or at least hints of them. Evelyne and Romain are certainly not disinterested in their attitude to Pierre, but nor are they exploitative. They in fact love him. Evelyne is sexually passionate towards him, but is also moved when she reads his letter to his mother; Romain professes platonic love, while projecting on to him a complex of class fantasy, nostalgia for youth and guilt (he stopped off for a rent-boy as he drove Pierre home the first night they met). In addition, the film contains two hints of alternative family arrangements or affective relationships. The lodging house has a kindly concierge, its boundaries are fluid – she cleans the room while he lies in bed and watches his television when hers is broken – and she has a gifted child with whom Pierre strikes up a friendship. And there is a memorable sequence in a bar when Pierre, seemingly at his happiest in the film apart from the brief idyll with Ingrid, dances around with

6 Jean-Michel Frodon calls this use of 'scope Téchiné's 'géographie des senti-ments' ('geography of feeling'): Frodon 1991.

a motley crew of Brazilian transvestites and the first rather seedy but now rather likeable punter he encountered.

Pierre either refuses these possibilities (as in his motto with the punters – 'j'embrasse pas, je ne suce pas, je ne me fais pas enculer'/'I don't kiss, I don't suck, I don't get fucked' – he lets nothing and no one penetrate him in the literal and figurative sense), or they are too evanescent and fragile to offer him anchor: the transvestites watch powerlessly as he is beaten and dragged away by the pimp and his henchmen. Pierre's desire is also, as ever in Téchiné (shades of *Souvenirs d'en France*), bound up with image. His desire for Ingrid, which had begun among the screens of a video arcade, is intensified for a second time when he glimpses her in the police van: his point of view shot sees her illuminated and shot very cinematically through the van windows, smoking and wearing red like a classic *femme fatale*. At various points in the film this kind of shot, as through or on to a screen, is used to fuel desire and/or to suggest distance: Pierre looks at Romain's television crew and guests in Spain, Ingrid in the shower at the sauna, which seems to help him overcome the sexual dysfunction of their first coupling, which had followed the only sequence of complicity and intimacy between them, in the Bois de Boulogne, shot for once in daylight. Significantly perhaps, these shots echo one from the very first sequence, when after he has left home his mother, grief-stricken by his departure, is photographed through a window, illuminated by a single light, suggesting that this is also part of Pierre's mental world.

Pierre's disarray in relation to the modern world he seeks to conquer is not just a question of emotional damage from the family and dominant codes of masculinity. *J'embrasse pas* is also very much a film about class. Pierre is tipped into the underclass and suffers considerable material want. But class difference also skews his relationship to Paris through his lack of cultural and educational capital: he is thus laughed at by the bourgeois students at the acting class, and is disempowered in relation to the world inhabited by Romain and Dimitri. He is unable to find a place in society other than through the physicality of prostitution and army (the lodging-house courtyard is a not a substitute for the working-class communities of 1930s French films), and he cannot see the advantages of his position. Romain's labelling him as 'l'enfant sauvage' ('the wild child'), one of several references in the film to Truffaut, makes him a catalyst for the debunking of certain bourgeois complacencies, and this is the source of some of the surprising but considerable humour of the film, in his gaze upon the bickering middle-class gay couple, or the concierge's reaction as he glimpses Romain's television interview with the Spanish writer: 'je change de chaîne?' ('shall I change channel?'). His youth parallels these ambivalences. His lack of all forms of capital means that he cannot see that Evelyne and Romain are equally if not more desperate than he is. Evelyne, who has had to nurse a paralysed mother and who is delighted by the taste of the sensual honey pot briefly offered by Pierre, is haunted by this proximity of death (she lost her father, and her mother dies during the film: the last time she sees Pierre she is wearing mourning clothes). She thus cannot handle Pierre's uncomprehending quotation to her of Hamlet's 'thousand natural shocks that flesh is heir to' (Act III, Scene I).

The narrative of youth, however, also enables processes of change and transformation, so that if the film constructs Pierre within the vectors of social and geographical origin, gender, and contemporary consumer capitalism, he is not determined by these. Society is also deterritorialising and plural, as we have seen, and the provisional and performative aspects of identity are here magnified by the youth of the main protagonist. The motif runs throughout the film, in the acting class, in Dimitri's 'number' at the dinner party as he acts the role of the older gay man. Even if the rehearsals to which Pierre submits himself in mirrors are in order to conform to a prearranged role, of rent boy or beggar, they are simply roles, a notion that extends to his general sense of self. Pierre is capable of change. By the end, he has swapped his previous incarnation of immaculate hairstyle, leather *blouson* and white tee-shirt for the shaven head and uniform of the French army. This is far from the teleology of a happy ending of social and institutional integration. There is a juxtaposition of brutality and vulnerability in the way he voices to an interviewing officer a desire for revenge, and also for the 'leap into the void' involved in parachuting at night. His performances in front of the mirror this time involve insults 'to toughen him up', but another recruit, the regiment's victim, points out that the real source of hurt lies in the memory of the emotional comforts, and lies, of childhood. At least Pierre is refusing here the role of torturer or bully. On release from his service, and about to leave once again for Paris and an open future, Pierre stops off at the beach and is filmed in long shot, happily splashing and swimming in the water, the image, isolating him in a near abstract space of sky, sea and sand, suggesting freedom and possibility and in direct contrast with the grids and bars of, for example, the Paris sequence discussed earlier. The scene is also of course reminiscent of the final sequences of Truffaut's *Les Quatre Cents Coups*, when Antoine Doinel (Jean-Pierre Léaud), having fled the reformatory, arrives at the beach and the camera captures him in freeze-frame. The open and ambiguous endings of both films denote social and fictional worlds which now have their meanings in acts of becoming. The blank canvas that ends *J'embrasse pas* therefore refers to another film, and *another story to come*.

Les Voleurs (1996)

If the structure of *J'embrasse pas* refers to the nineteenth-century novel, that of *Les Voleurs*, Téchiné's twelfth film, draws on the novel of twentieth-century modernism. Set in the Rhône-Alpes region, the film explores the emotional entanglements of a group of characters on both sides of the law. Alex (Daniel Auteuil) is a neurotic cop working in the deprived La Duchère district of Lyons, while his brother Ivan (Didier Bezace) and father Victor (Ivan Desny) run a criminal gang trafficking stolen cars. Alex becomes sexually involved with a young woman, Juliette (Laurence Côte), whom he had initially arrested for shoplifting. Her brother Jimmy (Benoît Magimel) is part of his family's gang and has served time in prison thanks to Alex. Juliette in turn is involved emotionally and sexually with a university philosophy professor, Marie (Catherine Deneuve). A heist at a railway marshalling yard goes disastrously wrong when Ivan is shot dead. Juliette, who had been coerced into participating, is the only one whose face is identified, but she had been mistaken for a man and builds a new life for herself in Marseilles. Alex and Marie develop a kind of friendship as they bid, from a distance, to protect her. Marie commits suicide, and Alex returns to his thankless job.

A plot summary fails, however, to render the film's complexity. The chronological narrative – in formalist terms the *fabula* or 'story' – is transformed by a plurality of time frames and narrative voices and viewpoints in the *syuzhet* or 'discourse', announced by a cacophony of voices (from the film's different voiceover narrations) over the opening credits. The film opens and closes with a prologue/epilogue centred on Justin (Julien Rivière), the young son of Ivan and his wife Mireille (Fabienne Babe). He awakes at night, in the family's mountain chalet on the morning of 4 February, to watch his father's body being brought home by the other gang members, and events, including the arrival of Alex – summoned by Ivan's wife Mireille against Victor's wishes – and of Juliette are narrated through his voiceover and his point of view. Six further narrative sections follow this pattern:

- that of Alex, beginning a year earlier with his first encounter with Juliette, and ending with the visit to the chalet;
- that of Marie, beginning with Juliette's visit to her on the evening of 4 February, when she makes one of her two suicide attempts in the film, and ending with Marie being driven home by one of Jimmy's associates, having failed to find Juliette;
- that of Juliette, beginning with the height of her love affair with Marie six months earlier, and ending with the disastrous heist;
- that of Justin, on 6 February, at Ivan's cremation, and particularly centred on his relationship with Alex;
- that of Alex, from 16 February to the summer, ending with Marie's suicide, his trip to Marseilles and his decision not to speak to the new, poised and confident Juliette;
- and Justin's epilogue, which also seems to take place that summer, and which again has him eavesdropping on adult conversations in the family house, with the closing shot of him in bed echoing that of the prologue, but in which a new relationship with Jimmy is portrayed.[7]

As Jonathan Rosenbaum has pointed out (Rosenbaum 1996), this fragmented narrative structure owes much to William Faulkner, a writer with a high profile in France since the 1930s.[8] *The Sound and the Fury* (1929), for example, unfolds over four days (though much more distanced in time than the chronology of *Les Voleurs*), beginning with the narration of the mentally handicapped Benjy, the character, analogous to Justin, who understands the least the events portrayed. The novel then moves backward in time eighteen years to his brother

---

7 The original ending, shown at Cannes, in which Justin fires on a mountain the pistol purloined in the prologue, was re-edited by Téchiné as it was interpreted by critics as unambiguously announcing a criminal future.

8 See for example the essays on him by Jean-Paul Sartre (Sartre 1947).

Quentin's point of view, then to that of a third brother Jason's point of view the day before Benjy's tale, then switches to third person narration for the day after. In both *The Sound and the Fury* and *Les Voleurs*, a central female character – Caddie and Juliette respectively – is loved obsessively by two of the narrators. Caddie has no narrative voice of her own except when it is embedded in that of another; Juliette has a chapter from her point of view but no voiceover. She is also loved of course by Jimmy, in a reworking of the brother–sister relationship, in minor key, from *Ma Saison préférée*.[9]

What this fragmentation achieves is an intensification of that cinema of sociality first evident in *Hôtel des Amériques*. That film's plurality of characters circulating round a central couple has transmuted into a work without a centre or periphery. Reuniting the Auteuil–Deneuve couple in the aftermath of the successful *Ma Saison préférée* (1993), it nonetheless places them within a galaxy of other characters and actors, and, certainly in the case of Auteuil, casts them against type: Alex, like everyone else in the film, is damaged, perverse, dislikeable. (Deneuve wields a certain amount of cultural capital as an academic, but she is deglamorised, and – taking advantage of a real-life accident during the shoot – spends much of her time on crutches: this fits in well with a film in which physical harm and bandaging are metaphors for the widespread emotional damage.) Even those figures who do not have their own 'chapter' – Mireille, Victor, Marie's former lover – hint at further stories to tell, so that the film's multiplicity is never exhausted. The central event of the film is of course the heist and Ivan's death. All the narrative chapters of *Les Voleurs* converge on the night and day of 4 February, a month which occupies the centre of the film's chronology, with Justin's stories as pivot. Juliette's and Alex's first chapter ends then, Marie's and Alex's second chapter begins. In some traditional uses of flashback, scenes in the past are used to establish or reveal some kind of explanatory 'truth', be it factual as in a crime or investigative film (*The Accused*, director J. Kaplan, 1988; *JFK*, director O. Stone, 1991), or psychological and emotional (*Midnight Cowboy*, director J. Schlesinger, 1969; *Sophie's Choice*, director A. J. Pakula, 1982, even *Tirez sur le pianiste*, director F. Truffaut, 1960). *Les Voleurs* is not so untraditional that it disrupts linearity or renders

9 *Les Voleurs* was also made in the wake of Tarantino's *Pulp Fiction* (1994), which Téchiné admired, although he has stated there was no conscious imitation: (Jousse, Lalanne, Strauss 1996: 35).

time periods indiscernible. But unlike in Truffaut, for example, the fragmented time scheme serves to emphasise relationality rather than causality. Like a stone thrown into a pond, Ivan's death exposes ripples of social interconnection and interaction: the concentric circles implicate families, gangs, characters who otherwise would never meet, and, by implication, ever wider social milieus. As Téchiné put it:

> Je voulais que le sens circule sans que personne ait le pouvoir, je voulais une vérité qui change de corps, de visage, de point de vue, qui se transforme et finit même par se perdre, emportée par le mouvement de vie qui continue. Même si c'est une histoire violente, il y a une autre violence, supérieure, celle du 'tout passe'.[10]

There is no 'last word' in Les Voleurs, and it certainly cannot be found, for example, in Marie's lectures and readings from Freud's Civilisation and Its Discontents. Typical of the film's pluralism, her intellectual position is neither validated nor invalidated, but always to be seen in relation to other stories and positions.

Téchiné is also able to achieve this through the juxtaposition of modernist techniques and genre cinema, precisely two genres, those of crime thriller and melodrama. A certain amount of documentary research went into the making of Les Voleurs, including advice from Michel Alexandre, the ex-police officer and writer on Bertrand Tavernier's L.627 (1992). The law–not law distinction, so crucial to the police genre, even and especially when lines are blurred by 'bent', weak or damaged cops, is somewhat sidestepped by Téchiné's technique. An Oedipal sexual economy proves elusive: Alex, like Marie, renounces the girl, continues in his choice of childlessness, and will carry on an unheroic and thankless task (the last shots of him at a crime scene focus on a row of hostile faces, with younger ones replacing the old). In any case he is not the centre of the film. The heist itself is now part of a French tradition dating back to the famous 28-minute music and dialogue-free sequence of Jules Dassin's Du rififi chez les hommes (1954). The heist in Les Voleurs has dialogue (arguments about who will drive off the first car, the crisis when the guards arrive), but no music, and its soundtrack emphasises above all the slow, ghostly

10 'I wanted meaning to circulate without anyone having any power, I wanted a truth which changed body, face and point of view, which transformed itself and even disappeared, carried off by the continuing movement of life. Even if it is a violent story, there is another, greater violence, that of "everything changes"' (Frodon 1996).

screech of moving railway wagons. The scene's austerity, abstraction, obliqueness, use of sound and focus on objective details recall Robert Bresson's techniques in *Un Condamné à mort s'est échappé* (1956), *Pickpocket* (1959) or indeed *L'Argent* (1983), in which there is a robbery scene.

Les Voleurs continues the melodramatic mode – the residual Brechtianism – of Téchiné's cinema in its exploration of power and patriarchal family relationships. This is magnified most notably by the presence in the film of the family house, presided over by Victor, its secrets and oppressions first mapped by Justin, his nocturnal explorations emphasising its dark, labyrinthine power, and also its affections and desires. Alex returns to it, briefly and reluctantly, a place he had to get out of. At the end, Jimmy *may* be gaining a place within it, and transforming it. The family home has reverberations visible in Alex's own, a meticulous and emotionless space: divorced, he lives alone, his sexual encounters with Juliette never take place there, his dinner invitation to Marie ends with him taking – stealing – a surreptitious photograph of her as she sleeps. Téchiné's combination of modernism and melodrama in this film is consistent with certain uses of Faulkner, for example Douglas Sirk's adaptation of *Pylon* (1934) in *Tarnished Angels* (1958), a tale of emotionally damaged characters whose contrastive aerial context – Robert Stack plays an ex- fighter pilot of the First World War dragging his family through a world of stunt races – is echoed in *Les Voleurs* in the glider glimpsed by Alex, Mireille and Justin on 4 February, and in the paragliders later observed by Alex and Justin, their blaze of colour in the azure juxtaposed with the sombre mood between the two individuals. Two sequences serve to illustrate how these techniques and references converge in *Les Voleurs* to form Téchiné's characteristic exploration of (power) structures and becoming, dystopia and utopia, through arrangements of cinematic space and time.

Justin's story, that which is neither prologue nor epilogue, begins at Ivan's cremation. On the soundtrack, there is only the sound of the coffin being placed in the incinerator and that of metal being closed. The camera pulls back from this process to reveal the congregation. Justin's voiceover is about the temperature and the fact that – 'fortunately' – no one is crying. A series of close-ups reveals the stony expressions of the main characters, while Justin makes an excuse ('pipi') to Victor and leaves, followed by Alex. The first conversation between them takes place in the snowy graveyard, in a shot–reverse shot set-up that emphasises the distance (that is, age and time) between them by the use of high and low angles (at one point Justin is sitting on the ground). Justin asks Alex how much he earns a month, he answers, and Justin is unimpressed. The camera then tracks them walking down the hill, their journey interrupted by a barrier descending and a train crossing the frame in the horizontal plane. There follows a cut to an immediately different scene, as the pair enter a small fairground on which is playing a pop song ('Douha Alia') by the Algerian musician Cheb Mami. Behind the standing, watching and smoking figure of Alex is a circular ride consisting of aerial craft, and behind that the mountains. In the foreground, an unsmiling Justin is driving a dodgem car. Then, at a shooting gallery, Justin successfully fires two shots, but when told by Alex it is time to leave he points the gun at him; Alex snatches it away. Alex catches up with Justin on the station platform. Justin sits down and weeps, the camera filming him at his level, and Alex, who stares, motionless, unable to comfort the boy, at his.

The sequence, which lasts just over four minutes, reiterates many of the film's preoccupations, not least in its references to money, guns and cars. As mature man and young boy confront each other in the frozen graveyard, the past weighs like a nightmare on the brains of the living – both the accumulated history of dead generations, and their own individual pasts. Justin, as damaged as anyone else in the film, is also Alex the former child, a relationship of simultaneous similarity and distance articulated by the camera angles, with the final implication that Alex is, and was, in the same distress as Julien, but that he cannot reach over the years to deal with it. The sequence continues to explore binaries of the inert and the mobile: the shot of a train which is more to do with barriers and closure than movement, the final shots, as in *Hôtel des Amériques*, beside a railway line, promising but far from guaranteeing departures; and the dodgem cars, used so famously in Carné's fatalistic *Le Quai des brumes* to denote 'static movement'. Needless to say – this is in the middle of the father and brother's funeral after all – the carnivalesque, barrier-subverting connotations of the fairground are here absent, as is the relentless de-psychologising play of surfaces and intensities to which the fairground motif is put in Fellini (see Deleuze 1985: 119; 1988: 89–90). Both Alex and Justin are stuck in a miserable interiority belied by the plethora of images of childhood in the background, as with the fluffy toys for the air-rifle scene. In particular, throughout the film Alex has been portrayed as trapped in structure, and bureaucracy, to the point of obsessional neurosis.

However, *Les Voleurs* is not a film about determinism.[11] Even at this dark point, connotations of childhood, movement and departure subsist. The dialogue between Alex and Justin, discussing the former's choice of profession, uses the French expression 'prendre le large', 'le large' meaning 'open sea'. By the end of the film, Alex has at least learned something emotionally from a relationship with Juliette that had begun with brutal, almost anonymous sex, and with Marie, under the influence of whose whisky he momentarily opens up and produces a rare smile. Juliette, referred to by Marie as 'un être de fuite' ('a being of flight or escape'), seems to be a new person, also proving Marie's earlier assertion that 'she had several lives in front of her'. Justin in the epilogue is forging a new relationship with Jimmy who, as they sit together in a beautiful alpine meadow, teaches him card tricks. Indeed, Jimmy's nervous fiddling with his card pack had throughout the film paralleled Justin's throwing and catching a tennis ball, a gesture famous in Freud as the *fort-da* game in which the child constructs its first narrative of lack and making good a lack (Freud 1955: 14–15). Jimmy's playful vocabulary here makes good the symbolic damage in the film associated with theft, as he asks who has 'stolen' a card, and 'finds' it, restores it, on Justin's person. Justin has at least the opportunity to recapture a childhood lost after recent traumas, but so does Jimmy. Significantly, Jimmy transports Justin home on his motorbike, a mode of transport that guarantees a (physical) intimacy that a car does not: the only other ride in the film to parallel this shot is that of Jimmy and Juliette, when the brother is attempting to comfort the sister after a suicide attempt by driving her out to the countryside. (An idyllic scooter ride in *Les Roseaux sauvages* has similar connotations.) While Justin in his voiceover expresses the belief (or wish) that Jimmy will become his mother Mireille's lover, this is by no means certain, given Jimmy's seemingly asexual or ambivalent behaviour in the film. The prospect of change for Jimmy

11 Téchiné: 'Un personnage n'est pas seulement un object produit par son milieu, c'est aussi un sujet qui exerce son désir dans un champ social' ('A character is not just an object produced by a milieu, he or she is also a subject exercising their desire in a social field': Frodon 1996).

is also there, in that Mireille is borrowing Justin's schoolbooks in order to help him with reading and writing. However, at the very least the Justin–Jimmy relationship represents, rather than *filiation*, vertically and hierarchically structured as in the traditional family, one of *alliance*, a horizontal connection between heterogeneities.

Jimmy had explicitly ruled out such a mode of transportation for Marie when she had come looking for Juliette. Instead, the task of driving Marie home through a dangerous area is entrusted to his accomplice Nabil (Naguime Bendidi), and the resulting car ride is one of the film's most memorable scenes, and one of its rare moments of humour. Throughout *Les Voleurs*, cars had had multiple connotations: as commodities, stolen, bought and sold; as emotional indices, for Juliette first seduced Alex in the front seat of his car, and the tensions between them are played out in the car journey they make to the chalet following Ivan's death; after which it is Victor who drives Justin to school, signalling a new part of his life; and there are the dodgems at the fair. Cars also *move*, and an aspiration to movement runs throughout the film; they also play a role in the film's narrative transitions, bringing people together, marking passages from one level of the story to another.

Nabil takes a long way round, and, after Marie's initial protests, asks for a 'philosophy lesson'. Téchiné's penchant for bringing together in his narratives heterogenous individuals here reaches its apogee, as the philosophy professor, the embodiment of cultural capital, shares a few moments with the *beur* gang member. The conversation is shot through the windscreen, the camera sometimes framing the two, sometimes one, but always establishing a relationship of equivalence. Initially nonplussed, Marie says she needs a subject that interests him: the response is, of course, money. Marie then launches herself into a disquisition on money, pointing out its negative connotations in philosophy, its political association with capitalism, and the Freudian metaphor of money = shit.[12] (It is the most explicit discussion of money in the film since the performance of 'Money Makes the World Go Around' from *Cabaret*, an obviousness rendered palatable by its being performed by a drag act.) Nabil not only disagrees with this negativity, needless to say, he counters Marie's high cultural discourse ('la représentation que vous avez de l'argent'/'the representation you

12 See for example Character and Anal Eroticism (1908); Freud 1977: 205–215.

make of money',[13] a youthful stealing of a book as 'le contraire de l'ivresse'/'anything but intoxicating' with his own popular language: 'les mecs ils sont givrés'/'they're crazy these blokes'). He then turns on the radio and sings along to Cheb Mami's 'Douha Alia', which then becomes a recurrent theme in the film, emerging again at the fairground and over the closing credits. However, this is not so much a confrontation as a juxtaposition. Marie and Nabil's linguistic terrains at least coincided on the use of the word 'merde'. And although the final musical moments represent his attempt to regain control of the situation, to shut her up in fact, he had of course provoked the clash of syllogisms here, and in their parallel, different ways the pair share an aesthetic moment thanks to the music, the abandonment of language, and the picturesque shots of Lyons by night which close the two-minute scene. He sings, she seems momentarily at peace (in serene, reflective facial expressions that nonetheless fall short of her tearful ecstasy when she takes Alex to see *The Magic Flute*), the car is poised between her home/territory and his.[14]

Despite the twenty years since *Souvenirs d'en France*, it is still possible to discern in *Les Voleurs* a powerful critique of bourgeois society and family, through a making aware of not only the structures the characters inhabit, but also the tactics they employ for finding ways through modernity. Diane Sippl, for example, uses Michel de Certeau's distinction between 'strategies' (institutional, spatial, abstract) and 'tactics' (dominated, fleeting, makeshift escapes from order) to describe Téchiné's characters as 'scavengers of emotions who use pockets of time to spin new webs of intersubjectivities' (Sippl 1997: 43). Some questions remain however: Téchiné has said in the accompanying DVD interview that Marie kills herself 'by exalta-tion'; in the film her suicide note (accompanying her *gift* to Alex of transcripts and tapes of interviews with Juliette) explains that in life we never renounce, merely replace, and that she is unwilling to replace Juliette. While there are many examples in Téchiné's work of life-affirming renunciation (Alex, arguably, in this film, Lili in *Le Lieu du crime* (1986)), the only other example of a suicide is that of

13 The English subtitles say, 'I don't understand how money figures for you'.
14 'S'il y a une utopie dans le cinéma de Téchiné, c'est bien celle qui consiste à mettre face à face les pires ennemis ou les individus les plus incompatibles' ('if there is a utopia in Téchiné's cinema, it's that which consists in putting worst enemies or the most incompatible individuals together') (Lalanne 1996).

Quentin in *Rendez-vous*. The neo-romantic discourse that embodied seems rather out of place in *Les Voleurs*. It must also be asked why Juliette is the one carrier of narrative who does not have her own voiceover. In her *Sight & Sound* review, Ginette Vincendeau makes the standard feminist critique of Juliette as *femme fatale*, object of desire for all protagonists, leading them – particularly Ivan and Marie –to perdition (Vincendeau 1998). However, Juliette is not punished in the film – far from it, her story seems to take the happiest turn – and she is more than a mere relay of others' looks of desire. Sippl, argues, for example, that Alex is at least partly changed by the end of the film by his contact with a 'world of women'. (Contrast the brutal sex scenes between Juliette and Alex, and the intimacy and serenity of the famous bath scene between Juliette and Marie, shot mostly in a mirror, underlining the alternative nature of their world; notably, the hotel bathroom as used by Alex is a dismal space of distance and separation from Juliette, as he eats his breakfast alone there.) And Vincendeau herself admits that Juliette does not fit the *femme fatale* bill in terms of looks and performance. Indeed, *Les Voleurs* is in part a film about gender performance, about gender as performance: in the transvestite show at the Mic-mac club, Juliette's dance in front of the stage at the meeting between Alex and Ivan, Alex's momentary first impression of Juliette as a boy, the gender category mistake around her presence at the heist. To investigate these questions further, it is necessary to focus in on Téchiné's distinctive treatment of the family, gender and sexuality.

References

Bakhtin, M. (1981). Discourse in the Novel, in *The Dialogic Imagination*, edited by M. Holquist, translated by C. Emerson and M. Holquist. Austin, University of Texas Press, 259–422.

Deleuze, G. (1985). *Cinéma 2: L'Image-Temps*. Paris, Minuit.

Deleuze, G. (1988). *Cinema 2: The Time-Image*, translated by H. Tomlinson and R. Galeta. London, Athlone Press.

Freud, S. (1955). *Beyond the Pleasure Principle, Group Psychology and Other Works. Standard Edition of Complete Psychological Works xviii (1920–1922)*, translated by J. Strachey. London, Hogarth Press.

Freud, S. (1977). *On Sexuality: Three Essays on the Theory of Sexuality and Other Works*, translated by J.Strachey. Harmondsworth, Penguin.

Frodon, J.-M. (1991). A hauteur d'homme, au rythme de l'émotion, André

Téchiné peint la beauté et la douleur des 'premières fois'. *Le Monde*, 22 November, 17.

Frodon, J.-M. (1996). André Téchiné mène la ronde des sentiments sur fond de film noir. *Le Monde*, 22 August, 16.

Harvey, S. (1978). *May '68 and Film Culture*. London, British Film Institute.

Jones, K. (1997). *André Téchiné: la estrategía de la tensión*. Valladolid: Semana internacional de cine.

Jousse, T. (1991). Illusions perdues. *Cahiers du cinéma*, 450 (December), 20–22.

Jousse, T. and F.Strauss. (1994). Entretien avec André Téchiné. *Cahiers du cinéma*, 481 (June), 12–17.

Jousse, T., J.-M. Lalanne and F. Strauss. (1996). Entretien avec André Téchiné. *Cahiers du cinéma*, 505 (September), 33–39.

Lalanne, J.-M. (1996). Comme une effraction. *Cahiers du cinéma*, 505 (September), 28–31.

Lapsley, R. and M. Westlake (1992). From *Casablanca* to *Pretty Woman*: the politics of romance. *Screen*, 33, 1 (spring), 27–49.

Lovell, T. (1980). *Pictures of Reality: Aesthetics, Politics and Pleasure*. London, British Film Institute.

MacCabe, C. (1981). Realism and the Cinema: Notes on Some Brechtian Theses, in T. Bennett, *et al.* (eds), *Popular Television and Film*. London, British Film Institute, 216–235.

Milne, T. (1986). *Rendez-vous*. *Monthly Film Bulletin*, 53, 633 (October) 318–319.

Moretti, F. (1987). *The Way of the World: The Bildungsroman in European Culture*. London,Verso.

Neale, S. (1981). Genre and Cinema, in T. Bennett, *et al.* (eds), *Popular Television and Film*. London, British Film Institute, 6–25.

Orr, C. (2000). Scenes from the Class Struggle in Sweden: *Persona* as Brechtian melodrama, in L. Michaels (ed.), *Ingmar Bergman's Persona*. Cambridge University Press, 86–109.

Pechey, G. (1989). On the Borders of Bakhtin: dialogisation, decolonisation, in K. Hirschkop and D.Shepherd (eds), *Bakhtin and Cultural Theory*. Manchester University Press, 39–67.

Philippon, A. (1983). L'Actor's Studio aux Amandiers. *Cahiers du cinéma*, 354 (December), V–VI (*Le Journal des Cahiers*).

Rosenbaum, J. (1996). Criminal Genius. *Chicago Reader*, 22 December. (www.chicagoreader.com/movies/archives/1296/12276.html)

Sainderichin, G.-P. and C.Tesson. (1982). Entretien avec André Téchiné. *Cahiers du cinéma*, 333 (March), 32–38.

Sartre, J.-P. (1947). Sartoris par W. Faulkner; A propos de *Le Bruit et la fureur*. La temporalité chez Faulkner, in Situations I. Paris, Gallimard, pp. 8–9 and 70–81.

Sedgwick, E.K. (1985). *Between Men: English Literature and Male Homosocial Desire*. New York, Columbia University Press.

Sippl, D. (1997). The Virtues of Theft: André Téchiné's *Thieves*. *CineAction*, 43, 42–49.

Téchiné, A. (1996). Le Dépaysement humain (Interview). *Nouvelle Revue Française*, 520 (May), 41–57.

Téchiné, A. (2004). *J'embrasse pas*. DVD Interview. Paris, Studio Canal.

Vincendeau, G. (1998). *Les Voleurs. Sight & Sound*, 8, 4 (April), 57.

Vincendeau, G. (2000). Juliette Binoche: The Face of Neo-romanticism, in *Stars and Stardom in French Cinema*. London, Continuum, 241–252.

1 The 'cross-heritage' movie: Roland Barthes and Marie-France Pisier in *Les Sœurs Brontë*

2 A utopian space before the catastrophe: Manuel Blanc in *J' embrasse pas*

3 Road to nowhere: Daniel Auteuil and Julien Rivière in *Les Voleurs*

4 André Téchiné directing Daniel Auteuil and Catherine Deneuve in *Ma Saison préférée*

5 A defamiliarising social whirl: Sandrine Bonnaire in *Les Innocents*

6 Alternative families and ghost-like personages: Gaspard Ulliel and Grégoire Leprince-Ringuet in *Les Egarés*

Families and sexualities

Le Lieu du crime (1986)

At the start of Téchiné's seventh feature, *Le Lieu du crime*, co-scripted with Pascal Bonitzer and Olivier Assayas, 13-year-old Thomas (Nicolas Giraudi) chances upon Martin (Wadeck Stanczak), an escaped convict hiding out in a cemetery near his home in rural south-west France. Martin demands money but later saves his life, stabbing his fellow-escapee Luc (Jean-Claude Adelin) when he tries to strangle Thomas. Martin falls in with Thomas's mother Lili (Catherine Deneuve), a forty-something divorcee who runs a night club by the river, and he offers her an escape from her stifling Catholic milieu and mother (Danielle Darrieux), and unhelpful ex-husband Maurice (Victor Lanoux). But their sexual escapade – its final consummation witnessed by Thomas who has run away from his Catholic boarding school – comes to an end one stormy night when Martin is shot and mortally wounded by the two convicts' aggrieved accomplice, Alice, who later commits suicide (Claire Nebout). Lili tells the police the truth, that Martin did not threaten her, and she is carted off in a police van, finally leaving the village.

On the surface, the film seems to invite a straightforward Freudian reading, with an 'incestuous' or excessively close relationship between mother and son that is then 'resolved' when Thomas finds his place in the sexual and social order, returning at the end to live with his father (who forbids Lili to see him but lets her observe from behind a curtain), and having his first conversations with him about love and sex. Thomas, an alienated and rebellious child, performs his own version of the family romance, in which, according to Freud's 1909 essay (Freud 1977: 217–225), the child's negotiation of the Oedipal trajectory, realising parental imperfections while retaining the earlier memory of their exalted status, passes through the fantasy of being a foundling, of different (nobler) birth. Thomas does this twice, telling Martin that his parents died in a car accident, and the priest (Jacques Nolot) that his real mother, not Lili, will claim him one day. Thomas finds his final 'place' via a relay of phallic symbols: the knife Thomas gives to Martin who then uses it to kill Luc, the gun Martin gives to Alice who then uses it to kill him, with Martin as momentary substitute father figure who finds a place in the mother's bed but is then eliminated.

Such a reading can be juxtaposed with the generic tendencies of *Le Lieu du crime*. Certainly, the embryonic crime movie it in part represents means that it is haunted by the law–not law distinction, and this in turn spills over into the film's central melodramatic mode. We should recall that melodrama was a response in the nineteenth century to the loss of the sacred and a symbolic crisis of social legitimacy, often therefore played out in dramas of patriarchal right from which identity emerges out of the crisis of family romance. Discussing Vincente Minnelli's films, Geoffrey Nowell-Smith writes:

> the Hollywood melodrama is ... fundamentally concerned with the child's problems of growing into a sexual identity within the family, under the aegis of a symbolic law which the father incarnates. What is at stake (also for socio-ideological reasons) is the survival of the family unit and the possibility for individuals of acquiring an identity which is also a place within the system, a place in which they can both be 'themselves' and 'at home', in which they can simultaneously enter, without contradiction, the symbolic order and bourgeois society. (Nowell-Smith 1987: 73)

However, as we saw in the previous chapter, the Brechtian and Sirkian elements of Téchiné's filmmaking mean that different sexual economies are explored. Despite Téchiné's typically pluralising technique, in which pairs and groups of heterogeneous characters are made and unmade throughout the film (including Alice and Thomas, unaware of the connection between them), it is above all Lili/Deneuve's film. The mode of melodrama is here very close to the 'woman's film' à la Cukor, in which the narrative is about problems confronting women in relation to sexuality and society.

Deneuve's first scene is when Thomas returns home after the first meeting with Martin. In fact she and the house, along with the teacher-priest who is expressing his concerns to her about the boy, are first observed by Thomas as he returns from the first meeting with Martin and from his grandparents' where his first communion is being prepared, and where in an argument Thomas had been struck by his father. The first shot of Deneuve is significant for two reasons. She is filmed on the doorstep, a literally liminal space between the oppositions of inside and outside, confinement and landscape, which characterise the film and which are intensified by the use of cinemascope and the filming of long shots and close-ups, including in this sequence. Lili never gets beyond the entrance to the garden in the sequence, and most of the time is filmed inside the house. The motif of enclosure in the film extends to the village itself, and the contrast with the sense of space provided by the landscape. One mid-shot from inside has Lili framed in the doorway as she returns from seeing off the priest, so that landscape and interior are caught in the same view. (When the whole family later gathers on the grandparents' terrace to eat the communion lunch, it is on a studio set, as strangely artificial as the terrace in Alain Resnais's *Providence*, and which emphasises confinement rather than the natural scene.) Second, Lili's dress is sober, a pale-blue cardigan in particular signifying a deglamorisation of her star persona which continues through this sequence – she discards it only in order to iron –and the film as a whole, culminating in the paddy wagon. Narrative expectation is aroused – as in *Hôtel des Amériques*, when, if at all, will she 'become Deneuve', that is autonomous and empowered socially and sexually? The first room of the house she enters is the kitchen, where, distressed about Thomas's story of false parenthood, she sits down. The voyeuristic aspect of the sequence has ended and the conversations between her and the now contrite Thomas take place in the cinemascope frame or in two-shots. From the kitchen Lili enters a room where she begins ironing, initially framed with her back to the mirrors on a wardrobe. In the previous scene, Thomas had been allowed a rehearsal in front of the mirror, familiar from Téchiné's other work, as he performed an aggressive speech against Martin. At this point in the film, Lili turns her back on identity scrutiny or that kind of adolescent becoming. She is filmed frontally as she performs the domestic work of ironing, in a manner reminiscent of the way Jeanne Moreau is filmed preparing her meal in *Souvenirs d'en France*, a Brechtian *gestus* foregrounding a whole history of women's work, with close-up inserts here of the details of her gestures which detain the nonetheless urgent narrative (Thomas is between two assignments with danger and perhaps death). Indeed, *Le Lieu du crime* revisits the familial and geographic terrain of that earlier film, but with the additional presence of a child and the massive presence of the landscape.

For this melodrama to take off into a more gothic intensity, however, there has to be an irruption of desire which goes beyond the mother–son or mother–daughter relation, as important as they are. Darrieux and Deneuve, the two greatest French female stars of their respective generations, had been cast by Téchiné in those roles for the aborted project of filming *Les Mots pour le dire*. In *Le Lieu du crime*, the mother–daughter dyad is the classic one of the struggle for differentiation on the part of the daughter from the traditional feminine destiny embodied by the mother. The mother is rather like Winnie in Samuel Beckett's *Happy Days*, obsessively mapping out the days, and life itself, with rituals and illusions of happiness. The key desire in the film comes of course from and towards Martin. Lili's first encounter with him is at her nightclub, where her persona is rather more empowered – and her dress business-like rather than either domestic or sexual – than at home and with Thomas. Unlike the previous interiors of the film, the club is bright, flashy, loud, almost vulgar. Jutting out into the Garonne river, its gaudy lights reflected in the water, it is also fantasmagoric, prefiguring for example the video arcades of *J'embrasse pas*. Lili lifts up the sweater of the unconscious Martin to see if the blood on it is his, desire and danger combined. The attraction for Martin will play itself out along the inside–outside, confinement–landscape opposition, with an intensity that tips over into the gothic, in ways reminiscent of the use of exteriors and interiors in *Les Sœurs Brontë*, contractions and magnifications of cinematic space and of emotion. The interplay between mental and physical landscapes, of the virtual and the real, means that this is also a film about ghosts and dreams: Martin is referred to as a ghost, deathly pale from his time in prison, sporting a white – unbuttoned – shirt for much of the film; the crucial encounters take place in a cemetery; Thomas for a while is unsure whether his experience has been, as Martin suggested to him, a dream. The two 'crimes' of the film – the attempted murder of Thomas and the killing of Luc – thus acquire a kind of archetypal or mythical status, founding events for what is to come, and are recounted in flashback. The child's early discovery of a criminal in a churchyard, and the social exploration of the law–not law distinction, call to mind Dickens' *Great Expectations* and David Lean's 1946 film version.[1] Here we have a specifically French gothic, with the boundaries of home–not home played out not only in relation to 'a house', but to the mysteries of the countryside at the frontier of the village (see Bonnet 1986).

The nightclub scene contrasts with the previous one at the home of the conservative ex-husband Maurice, which was similarly bathed in flickering lights, but from an 8mm home movie projector relaying images, even on to the bodies of the ex-spouses, of the past: this is a backward-looking desire, imposing grids. Attempting to retrieve the past relationship, Maurice lay on top of Lili, caressing her neck. After a transition provided by seascapes from the home movies, there is a cut to Thomas rubbing *his* neck and regaining consciousness from the assault by Luc. This marks a turning point in the film, in that from now on everything that has happened to Thomas will happen to Lili. On her return home from finding Martin a hotel, she brushes her hair in front of a mirror. She goes to the cemetery, and there is exactly the same sudden and slightly mysterious cut, possibly suggesting the entry into a fantasy world, which had accompanied Thomas from the moment he put down his bike to an extreme long shot of him walking to the right of frame across the field to the churchyard. There, Luc is being buried. Lili is shot from behind, through a passageway which leads into the sunlight, in exactly the opposite procedure from the earlier sequence when she re-entered her house. Martin runs after Lili just as Luc had pursued Thomas, but, as Martin had done with Thomas, to protect her from his accomplice, in this case Alice.

These considerations make it difficult to insert *Le Lieu du crime* into a master Freudian narrative. As is frequent in Téchiné, father figures are either discredited (Maurice, the priest), or absent (the grandfather, played by Jean Bousquet, has a hearing-aid and uses his deafness, and his fishing, to blot out the world). Whereas the Oedipus complex

1 To make a slightly less obvious comparison, the children's discovery of the escaped Republican prisoner at the beginning of Victor Erice's *El Espíritu de la colmena/The Spirit of the Beehive* (1973) is played out via the confines of middle-class family life, the sweeping landscapes of the Castilian plain, and the fantasmatic projections of the Frankenstein myth.

posits a frontier between childhood and adulthood, Téchiné is interested in the continuities between the two.[2] In a strict Freudian sense, Lili regresses, there is a 'becoming-adolescent' as she becomes open to change and rebellion. Thomas becomes more 'adult'. The object of desire in the film is Martin, for Lili and for Alice, but possibly also for Thomas. Thomas and Lili exchange, not phallic symbols, but dreams and fantasies. The ending is catastrophic for neither of them: Thomas is still distant from his father, he needed distance from his mother, the last shot of him, like the first, is of him cycling in the countryside; Lili's 'sacrifice' is an assertion of self, not a Bressonian renunciation.

As Lili herself puts it, 'se sauver ou se perdre c'est la même chose' ('it's the same thing to save or lose yourself'). *Se sauver* in French also means to flee, and the itineraries of both Thomas and Lili can be seen, to use a Deleuzean term, as lines of flight. Rather than the classic narrative teleology of the discovery of a true or authentic 'self', the emphasis here is on an endless process of becoming something else. Téchiné's construction of alternative sexual economies based on heterogeneities and alliances is partly dependent on the crisis or indeed absence of truth claims, such as those which might emanate from the church or the family (or Freud), and these new arrangements are set in motion by lies. Martin is obviously the catalyst for this, as intruder and impostor, disrupting fixed social positions, setting the narrative in motion. But in fact it is Thomas who is the great prankster and storyteller. The Victorian morality tale of the boy who cries wolf is here turned on its head. Thomas has an undeveloped sense of truth and falsehood because the adult world seems so boring and artificial, its 'truths' invalidated. The fantasmagorical aspect of the film, the mobile relay of desire, and the undermining of the boundary between childhood–adolescence and adulthood mean that characters in the film are both persons and particles, socially and historically delineated entities but also clusters of forces and possibilities which are not reducible to the individual.

---

2 'Ce qui m'intéresse, c'est toujours d'essayer d'entendre la voix de l'enfant jusqu'au cœur de l'adulte'('What interests me is always to try to hear the voice of the child in the heart of the adult'): Lalanne and Roth-Bettoni 1994.

Ma Saison préférée (1993)

Ma Saison préférée, co-scripted with Pascal Bonitzer, provided Téchiné with his biggest box-office success, with 1.1 million tickets sold in France, a more than reasonable score for the more art-house end of French cinema (but well behind for example Catherine Deneuve's biggest audience successes, Truffaut's *Le Dernier Métro* of 1980, with 3.4 million spectators, or François Ozon's *8 Femmes* of 2002, with 3.8 million, although the latter is much more of an ensemble piece). Like *Le Lieu du crime* but in a more sustained fashion, *Ma Saison préférée* seeks to portray three generations of the same family. Divided into four chapters ('Départ', 'Le Faux Pas', 'Le Pas suivant' and 'Le Retour') corresponding to the four seasons, it begins with the elderly widow Berthe (Marthe Villalonga) leaving her house in the countryside to move in with her daughter Emilie (Catherine Deneuve) and son-in-law Bruno (Jean-Pierre Bouvier), who share a legal practice and have two children, Anne, a university student (Chiara Mastroianni, Deneuve's own daughter) and an adopted teenage son, Lucien (Anthony Prada). Emilie re-establishes contact with her unmarried younger brother Antoine (Daniel Auteuil), a neurosurgeon in Toulouse, who has been estranged because of mutual antipathy between him and Bruno. A Christmas dinner with the whole family, including their secretary Rhadija (Carmen Chaplin), ends in a punch-up between Bruno and Antoine, who leaves with Berthe. As a result, Emilie and Bruno separate, and Emilie and Antoine renegotiate their relationship. Berthe's deteriorating condition leads to her moving into an old folks' home, and then her death. This is followed by a more impromptu family meal around the swimming pool: Emilie and Bruno are back together; Emilie declares publicly her love for Antoine.

Ma Saison préférée is the most Bergmanesque of Téchiné's films, in its emphasis on relationships rather than plot, its extensive use of close-ups, and its obsession with time. Indeed, the poem Emilie recites in the final scene is the same used in the lunch scene in *Wild Strawberries* (1957), but here given a very secularising and personal twist.[3] The technique of having the older character participate in

---

3 In the Bergman film, the poem is quoted during a discussion about religion. In fact it is a hymn, 'Where Is the Friend?', written by an archbishop in the Swedish church, Johan Olof Wallin (1779–1839): 'Mais où est donc l'ami que partout je cherche/Dès le jour naissant mon désir ne fait que croître/Et quand la nuit s'efface c'est en vain que j'appelle/Je vois ses traces, je sais qu'il est présent/

fantasy scenes from childhood – as when Emilie discusses with her parents the imminent birth of a younger brother – is also indebted to this film. However, the title indicates, as ever in Téchiné, the interplay between personal ('ma') and collective (natural and social) dimensions. At the final meal around the swimming pool, and just after the funeral, each character is asked to name their favourite season. As Kent Jones puts it,

> The film is not a 'family drama' nor a 'portrait of the French middle classes', but the exploration of a series of circumstances – related to family, society, generation, culture, geographical milieu – and the form in which a concrete group of people from three different age groups react to these circumstances. (Jones 1997: 117)

Those 'circumstances' – as ever in Téchiné, fundamentally ambivalent, determinant but not determining, both negatively and positively evaluated – are a constant presence in the film. In the opening sequence, Emilie and Bruno's car is dwarfed by the countryside, as it is filmed with its roof barely visible, wending its way down a road between crops. The relations with the mother are not only affective, they are spatial (rural and suburban–urban) and historical (peasant and 'modern'), as well as eloquent about old age and death in general. The young people in the film are simultaneously (over)coded as 'young' – beautiful male and female bodies displayed, indifference to the older generations – and also mysterious: Anne the possibly frustrated artist, experimenting with her sexuality, potentially, with Rhadija; Lucien the oversexed adopted son, fighting his own demons over that issue. It is left of course to those in the middle fully to articulate the mesh of all that determines what they are, and what they might still become, so the film is fundamentally about the two stars (since his role as Ugolin in *Jean de Florette* of 1986 Daniel Auteuil had emerged as one of France's most important male leads), and about the brother–sister relationship.

As Téchiné has himself pointed out, this relationship is very under-

---

Je sens qu'il est présent partout où la sève monte de la terre/Ou embaume une fleur, et où s'incline le blé doré/Je le sens dans l'air léger dans le souffle d'une caresse/Et que je respire avec délice/Et j'entends sa voix qui se mêle au chant de l'été'; in *Wild Strawberries*: 'where is the friend I seek at break of day?/When night falls I still have not found Him/My burning heat shows me His traces/I see His traces whenever flowers bloom/His love is mingled with every air'.

theorised and underrepresented, and it raises further challenges to orthodox Freudian theory:

> je me suis décidé pour un sujet qui me tenait à cœur, cette histoire de frère et sœur. Le cinéma, si prolixe sur les rapports entre mari et femme, ne s'intéresse guère à cette relation. Les frères et les sœurs sont les grands exclus du roman familial. (Frodon 1993)[4]

The Oedipal narratives of most Hollywood and other cinemas are based on a teleology of adult heterosexual love. Brother–sister narratives are abundant when young children are involved, with movies aiming to federate audiences of male and female children (*Mary Poppins*, director Robert Stephenson, 1964), and drawing on archetypes in fairy stories in their attempts to do so (the most famous European example being *Hansel and Gretel*). Those dealing with adult brother-sister relationships are extremely rare, and some yield to the temptation of incest narratives and the pull of heterosexual 'normality' (so that the brother–sister dimension is simply another obstacle required by the romance genre): *Close My Eyes* (Stephen Poliakoff, 1991), starring Clive Owen and Saskia Reeves, even *Cat People* (Paul Schrader, 1982), with Malcolm McDowell and Nastassja Kinski.[5] In the 1970s BBC TV sitcom *Sykes*, in which a middle-aged brother and sister live together, Hattie Jacques is there to provide a feminine but non-sexual and non-threatening foil to the eponymous writer and star. In the Hollywood action movie *Vertical Limit* (Martin Campbell/ Columbia Pictures, 2000), Chris O'Donnell has to rescue his sister from a mountain, but this is embedded in an Oedipal narrative of a dead father whose sacrifice had been a source of conflict between them. Among the rare exceptions to this pattern in American cinema,

---

4 'I decided upon a subject close to my heart, the brother–sister story. Cinema treats the husband–wife relationship in abundance, but is not interested in this. Brothers and sisters are the major exclusions from the family romance'. Téchiné adds: 'Je m'intéresse aussi aux célibataires, ce monde des solitaires et des solitudes qui sont à la fois choisies et contestées. Je m'intéresse aux gens qui n'arrivent plus à s'identifier à leur famille, qui n'arrivent plus à jouer le rôle que la société leur impose' ('I'm also interested in single people, the world of solitaries and solitudes that are simultaneously chosen and contested. I'm interested in people who no longer identify with their family, who can't play the role society imposes on them').

5 Some critics have not resisted this pull when looking at *Ma Saison préférée*: Amy Taubin wrote of the 'incestuous longing' that characterises the relationship (Taubin 1996).

and these are from the independent sector, are *Love Streams* (John Cassavetes, 1984) in which the siblings are played by the director and Gena Rowlands, and *You Can Count On Me* (Kenneth Lonergan, 2000), with its indirect *hommage* to Téchiné (use of Bach's G Major suite for solo cello as in *J'embrasse pas* and *Alice et Martin*). Whereas in Lonergan's film the siblings' relationship is dominated by the death of their parents when they were children, in Cassavetes the relationship is not based on backward-looking interdictions but is transformative and mobile, generating new ethical ways of being in the world and relating to others (Lardeau 1985).

The Freudian scenario writes out infantile attachments other than to the parents or parental figures, and its central Oedipal narrative emphasises the teleology and normality of adult genital heterosexual relations, and the strict separation of childhood and adulthood, transgression of which is punished by neurosis. As we have seen, Téchiné's films sidestep this scenario in favour of pluralism. Indeed, *Les Sœurs Brontë* had constructed a 'sororal' rather than Oedipal pattern of desire, and Téchiné's choice of Emilie for the name of the sister is no doubt a reference to that. In *Les Voleurs*, the relationship between Jimmy and Juliette takes centre stage on one occasion, and adds breadth and depth to the array of affectivities represented in the film. The brother–sister relationship in *Ma Saison préférée* works on several levels. First, while Emilie and Antoine are fully installed in adulthood in a social and professional sense, they, and by implication everyone, can never leave childhood behind emotionally. The opening credits pan across a painting – in fact an anonymous 'scientific' rendering that Téchiné discovered in an antiques shop in Toulouse – of conjoined twins, emphasising at the outset the indissolubility of childhood bonds. The film asks how these can be lived in adult life. Second, that indissolubility is also about a detachment from maternal and paternal bonds, or at least a relativisation of them. The nature of adult life, it is made clear, is one characterised by modernity. (This is made all the more tangible because of the contrasts set up between Antoine's rational–scientific persona – and the technology of the hospital – and the manifestations of a mysterious pre-modernity, as when Berthe in her later delirium successfully predicts an accident to Antoine and lightning striking the roof of her house.) The standard anti-Oedipal argument from Deleuze and Guattari is that the instrumentalism of modern capitalism depends on the death of the child in everyone

(Deleuze and Guattari 1972). *Ma Saison préférée*, not least because of the 'modernising' trajectory lived by the rural family, is full of representations and discussions of modern life and its consequence for relationships: solitude, conversations with oneself (Antoine twice *rehearsing* in the toilets conversations with Emilie or the family, Berthe muttering to herself as she sits alone) or often by the side of a road with cars hurtling past; Antoine himself, in a conversation in a car with Emilie, bemoans this:

> Energie, performance, action. Toute cette énergie partout c'est terrifiant. On n'a plus rien à faire enfin, intérieurement je veux dire et finalement même extérieurement. Donner un sens à ce qu'on fait c'est une autre paire de manches.[6]

In *Sibling Love: The Brother–Sister Culture in Nineteenth-Century Literature From Austen to Woolf*, Valerie Sanders explores the various representations of the relationship, of which two in particular are useful here. In Jane Austen, the brother-figure offers a template of masculinity – domestic, complicit – which proposes new standards of masculinity for prospective husbands. Certainly, the wayward and emotional Antoine is much more interesting than the solid if handsome Bruno, and, significantly, Emilie's 'choice' of the latter links with another aspect of the sibling relationship, that of different possible destinies that may be interchangeable, or else bounded, in nineteenth-century society at least, by rules of sexual difference. Charlotte Brontë's *The Professor*, and Branwell Brontë's 'Caroline' poems, demonstrate the ways in which Victorian brothers probe the implications of being their own sister, and sisters the implications of being their own brother, so that there is 'an interrogation of how their experiences would have been different had they been of the opposite sex' (Sanders 2004: 139). This is precisely a dimension of *Ma Saison préférée*, in which Emilie had abandoned ambitions of becoming a dancer in favour of her relationship with Bruno. This adds a virtual aspect to the film's realism, as we shall see, as the characters envisage other possible worlds:

> Dans *Ma Saison préférée*, Catherine Deneuve se rend compte que sa volonté d'être adulte était un rêve auquel elle n'a rien compris. Et le

6 'Energy, performance, action, all this energy everywhere is terrifying. We've got nothing to do really, internally I mean, and in the end even externally. Giving meaning to what we do is another story'.

personnage de son frère lui tend un miroir dangereux. Elle a peur de lui. Comme dit Cathy de Heathcliff dans *les Hauts de Hurlevent*: 'Il est encore plus moi-même que je le suis'. C'est pourquoi ce lien avec son frère est beaucoup plus fort qu'avec son mari ou avec la famille qu'elle s'est fabriquée. Cela la touche au plus profond de son identité.[7]

Ma Saison préférée's obsession with time is linked to this child-hood-middle age-death structure. Frequently referenced by inserts of still photographs (Emilie's first visit to Antoine, Antoine at Berthe's family house, a beautiful scene in which Berthe collapses in a cherry orchard in full fruit, and awakens gazing at the sky), and representations of water, it is dramatised by Emilie shattering an antique clock in the aftermath of the Christmas dinner (Antoine had done the same at a previous meal). The sequence in which the siblings transport Berthe to the old folks' home is eloquent of Téchiné's procedure.

Beginning with a mid-shot on Berthe as she stands in the family house behind the door, well dressed in a suit and not at first answering Emilie's knock, it traces a portrait of the house and her existence there via the trope of departure. For the siblings, it is also briefly a journey to the past, emphasised by the way in which, in long shots, they are dwarfed by the old-fashioned decor and cast in the house's pale brown light. Emilie hesitates at the door of the living room, ambivalent about the past, guilty about the old folks' home. After having to sit down because of 'the emotion', Berthe strides ahead, a long tracking shot, silent except for her steps, following her out of the house and ending with her closing the car door on herself. A medium close-up reveals her tears. In shadow, Emilie and Antoine close the shutters of the house, the soundtrack again limited to this action so redolent of finality. A point of view shot has Antoine momentarily gazing out at the cherry tree on which the camera lingers, a gaze that is also of course inward. Emilie discovers that Berthe has cut the throats of the chickens she kept. There follows a series of shots of the car as it negotiates the country roads and the south-western landscapes bathed in summer sunlight; a pause at a roadside café delivers awkward conversation

---

7 'In *Ma Saison préférée*, Catherine Deneuve realises that her wish to be an adult was a clueless dream. And the character of her brother holds a dangerous mirror up to her life. She is afraid of him. As Cathy said of Heathcliff in *Wuthering Heights*, 'he is more myself than I am'. This is why the link with her brother is much stronger than with the family she has made for herself. It touches the deepest part of her identity': interview with Téchiné (Frodon 1993).

and the noise of passing cars. The trio decide to revisit localities from their past. Walking in the woods, Berthe reminisces about the father and his agricultural equipment business; Antoine strips naked 'to fulfil an old childhood dream', swim in a river forbidden to them when they were young. The sequence ends with three shots of the trio in the car, Antoine driving, Emilie in the passenger seat, Berthe in the back. Berthe refuses flowers from Emilie as she does not want to be conspicuous when she enters the home. Emilie and Antoine exchange glances. Berthe reminds them of their habit of singing in the car when they were children, and the camera position changes to a shot of Berthe from the side of the car, the trees reflected in the window. Antoine and Emilie are singing a song from childhood, 'Les trappeurs de l'Alaska' (made famous by the *variétés* singers Mario Moro and Patrice Paganessi), Berthe is visibly moved and amused; the camera position changes so that all three of them can be seen. These two shots last 45 seconds and summarise the complexity of the treatment of time in the film. The car is moving forward, towards Berthe's future in the home (and to her death), moving away from the family house which began the sequence, and the past it represents. But at the same time, the reflected trees are seen to be moving backwards, back towards that past. In the car itself, the older generation is at the back, nearest that 'past', but the two younger people have regressed to childhood, so that the car momentarily becomes a capsule of past time, but with the seating positions transformed. The polyvalent treatment of time in these two shots emphasises the interpenetration of past, present and future, here joyous if ambivalent (given the nature of the journey), at other points in the film a source of disorientation and loss. The shot is also supremely cinematic, its movement reproducing the passing of a film reel through a camera or projector, its content mirroring cinema's capacity of recording both past time and movement itself. The breaking into song recalls those moments in musicals when characters are swept into a different world, a virtual world (of fantasy, here of memory), that shadows the real. These shots are later echoed when Antoine and Emilie take Berthe away from the home, but this time in rainstorm and in silence.

Elsewhere, being lost in time amounts to a confusion of the actual and virtual. Antoine puts Emilie up at his flat while he is on night shift, and then goes to see the young people at a bar. Suddenly, attention turns to a much older woman (in fact the torch singer Ingrid

Caven), the camera slowly zooms upon her as she starts singing a lament for past time: 'Le temps passera, tout ça s'effacera... je ne serai plus là' ('Time will pass, the end is nigh...Soon I'll die').[8] She continues to sing as she is escorted out in slow motion, watched by Antoine and the assembled beautiful young people. (Later, a montage of shots photographs the patients at the old folks' home, in contrastive fashion.) Antoine's expression is one of introspection, and then a sudden editing cut and slightly closer camera position has him awaking as if from reverie, having lost track of time. He runs to return to Emilie, a blurred tracking shot following him from the side, and from right to left, as he crosses a bridge at dawn. This 'backward' movement is accompanied on the soundtrack by the sound of church bells – a motif of traditional rural life also very present in *Le Lieu du crime* – but *played backwards*, a procedure which contributes to the rather fantastic elements of the sequence, as if Antoine was running on the spot as in a nightmare.[9] That shot is preceded and followed by him asking someone for the time, he doesn't wear a watch. The fact that Antoine is lost in time is confirmed when he arrives home, and in a fantasy sequence imagines that Emilie has thrown herself out of the window. As the image of her bloodied body on the pavement below fades into black and white, the next shot has Emilie waking to the sound of an alarm clock, watched by Antoine. The next shot, from his point of view, is of a still photo of them in their late teens or twenties. This ends part three of the film, and begins part four, the polyvalently titled 'Return': Berthe's deterioration and death, crises between Emilie – who moves back in with Bruno – and Antoine as she believes he could have saved her had she been treated earlier. The final scene, filmed as the sun sets, and reuniting the family around an impromptu meal, keeps alive the film's and characters' ambiguities, but here Emilie surprisingly steps out of the group. Here, in close-up, she recites the poem 'Où est donc l'ami que je cherche?', which becomes a love poem for Antoine as she explains that she recited it to herself as she was waiting to rejoin him in the summer after

8 Ingrid Caven, born in the German Saarland in 1938, was married to Rainer Werner Fassbinder. Her traversal of the counter-cultural artistic circles of France and Germany from the 1960s onwards is recounted in the Goncourt prize-winning novel by her current husband, Jean-Jacques Schuhl (Schuhl 2000).

9 The mechanics of the decision by Téchiné and his collaborators Martine Giordano (editor) and Michel Klochendler (sound editor), made in the sound-mixing studio, to use the bells in this way is recounted in de Baecque 1993.

boarding school. It is one of the most memorable moments, instants, of the mature Deneuve cinematic persona. Emilie, as throughout the film, continues to be dressed very soberly, here in white blouse and light-brown cardigan. The camera moves past Antoine's shoulder to frame her head in the evening light, and then profiles her from her left. It then silently pans back to Antoine's reaction shot, holding him in frame for seven seconds. The troubled Emilie has certainly not 'become Deneuve', nor has she engaged in that line of flight taken by the more adventurous Lili in *Le Lieu du crime*. The 'star turn' represented by her recitation can be contrasted with her final bow in *Le Dernier Métro*, in which the voyeuristic gaze of which she was so often the object in that film becomes a fetishising one, simultaneously maintaining and seeking to abolish distance, perpetuating woman as Other. By working outside such an Oedipal economy and its reliance on a heterosexual male gaze, Téchiné is able to play with Deneuve's star persona and to harness her subtle acting style to draw on ambivalences of emotion and restraint, to explore identification, and to establish equivalences between the male and female siblings. If anything, the 'becoming-Deneuve' of these stories of frustrated and unhappy cardigan-wearing women is part of Téchiné's interest in the actual and virtual, whereby the star persona, in a manner analogous to the fantasy sequences in the film or the alternative destinies of brother and sister, becomes a virtual shadow of the diegetic protagonist.

Les Roseaux sauvages (1994)

There is one other dimension to the brother–sister relationship in *Ma Saison préférée*. The heterosexual bias of Hollywood cinema and the wider culture means that it has difficulty in imagining and representing non-sexual friendships between men and women (the very basis of course of the comedy *When Harry Met Sally*, director Rob Reiner, 1989), and this largely explains the relative paucity of adult brother–sister narratives. That bias also writes out the possible 'solution', namely that the brother and sister, or friends, have different sexual orientations anyway. There is much autobiography in *Ma Saison préférée*, and, in Téchiné's next film, *Les Roseaux sauvages*, that element became explicit. Along with other directors, Téchiné was commissioned by Chantal Poupaud at the production company IMA, working with the arts TV channel la SEPT, to make a 50-minute film about his adolescence for the series *Tous les garçons et le filles de leur âge*. Extended into a full-length feature, *Les Roseaux sauvages* was shown at the 1994 Cannes Film Festival, along with two other films from the series, Olivier Assayas' *L'Eau froide* and Cédric Kahn's *Trop de bonheur*.

Les Roseaux sauvages was not a 'coming-out' film as such, although because of it – and also *J'embrasse pas* which coincided with the vogue of 'New Queer Cinema' early in the decade – Téchiné in the 1990s entered a kind of international pantheon of gay art cinema directors, with a film like *Les Voleurs* taking its place within Lesbian and Gay Film Festivals, as in London in 1998. Before tackling *Les Roseaux sauvages*, whose critical success extended to it sweeping the Césars for best film, best director and best female newcomer, it is useful to comment on the ways in which same-sex desire has been handled in Téchiné's cinema up to that point. It is tempting to see the general *décrispation* we noted in *Hôtel des Amériques*, and its relaxed but explicit treatment of gay desire, as linked to the changing profile of gay politics and culture in France. *Barocco* is very much a film about the closet; its blackmail plot hinges on allegations of homosexuality.[10] In that film, the references to other films were to an extent more 'loving' than the portrayal of Depardieu's body. The renewal of the feminist and gay movements in 1970s France, in the wake of May 1968, took place in what, under the presidency of Valéry Giscard d'Estaing, remained a largely conservative moral climate, despite advances such as the legalisation of abortion in 1974. For example, until 1979 Paris lacked the presence of visible gay bars that had begun to characterise other major western cities. With the election of François Mitterrand in 1981, and the equalisation of the age of consent in 1982, the way was laid for an increasing visibility and commercialisation of gay culture in France.[11]

However, straightforward 'gay' or 'queer' appropriations are highly problematic in the case of Téchiné. In being so, they shed light on what we might understand 'gay cinema' to be, and on the contributions the cultural specificities of the French and Anglo-Saxon worlds

10 As, arguably, is *Paulina s'en va*, the incest narrative a possible displacement of homosexual preoccupations, as in the Cocteau/Melville *Les Enfants terribles*.

11 However, Jacques Nolot has suggested in a radio interview that the greater explicitness in Téchiné of references to homosexuality is linked to the death of his mother: *Ciné Club* 1998.

make to that problematic. Lesbian and gay film festivals tend to be vehicles for two kinds of relationship to gay identity in productive tension with one another, relationships which following Deleuze and Guattari (1975/1989, 1980/1988) I will call major and minor: 'major' would be a tendency towards a fixed and finished notion of (gay) identity whose political expedience risked creating new closures, ghettos, territories and obligations; 'minor' would emphasise all that is unfixed and unfinished in the category, and stress its capacity for invention, becoming, proliferation of the new, and the undermining of dominant, in this case heterosexual culture's pretensions to the natural, normal and universal. (The same dichotomies could be set up for 'queer' – a funkier form of identity, or a creative, open-ended upsetting and transgression, as in its verbal form, 'queering'.) Téchiné's films, as we have seen, nearly always include at least a hint of same-sex activity, often in surprising contexts (Anne's 'chaste' advances to her brother's girlfriend in *Ma Saison préférée*), and many feature characters who either identify as gay (Luc in *Hôtel des Amériques*) or who engage in same-sex acts (Marie in *Les Voleurs*). Moreover, they always feature a cute young man, and not only that but, in ways which break with forms of spectatorship in popular cinema which eroticise the male body but only within certain limits, for example as phallus-bearing action heroes whose bodies are tested, they are cute men to be looked at. The bodies of Wadeck Stanczak in *Rendez-vous* and especially *Le Lieu du crime*, Simon de la Brosse and Abdel Kechiche in *Les Innocents*, Manuel Blanc in *J'embrasse pas*, Anthony Prada in *Ma Saison préférée*, Stéphane Rideau in *Les Roseaux sauvages* and *Loin*, Benoît Magimel in *Les Voleurs*, Alexis Loret in *Alice et Martin*, Gaspard Ulliel in *Les Egarés*, are all put on display, and are invariably objects of desire – and recipients of point of view shots – of other protagonists. However, Téchiné's films are neither militantly gay nor even coalesce around relatively fixed positions of gay identity and community. In this, Téchiné is, it could be argued, very much part of a French tradition of reticence towards identity politics. This reticence finds expression both in the republican tradition since 1789 which emphasises the relationship between the individual and the state, and to an extent amongst those gay theorists whose whole *raison d'être* is an opposition to that state system, for example Michel Foucault and Guy Hocquenghem.[12]

12 See Marshall 1996 and 2000.

Indeed, in an interview he gave in 1984 to the gay intellectual journal *Masques*, Téchiné is very Foucauldian in his analysis of contemporary 'liberations'. Resisting the 'reductive' notion that Branwell Brontë's life can be explained by homosexuality, he adds:

> On vit dans une époque d'importante émancipation sexuelle... et le travail du refoulement n'est pas forcément un travail négatif. Je crois que d'une certaine façon, ce qu'on libère quelque part, on l'écrase ailleurs. Il y a toujours un mouvement de balancier. (Dubar and Joecker 1984: 93)[13]

We have seen how for Téchiné characters are always unfinished entities, that their 'apprenticeships' never end, and that they constantly become 'strangers to themselves'. We have also seen the oscillation between the actual and virtual, place or no place (u-topia) which characterises his films. 'Utopia' was the word Guy Hocquenghem used in an article in *Masques* in 1985, 'Où en est l'homosexualité en 85, ou pourquoi je ne veux pas être un 'écrivain gay', to evoke the impoverishment such a label affords (literature then loses its 'utopie') (Hocquenghem 1985). And in one of his last articles, 'L'Homosexualité est-elle un vice guérissable?', published in *Gai-Pied Hebdo* in 1987, he argued for non-differentiation rather than the assertion of gay identity, and for the radical potential of 'not being able to tell' someone's sexuality (Hocquenghem 1987).[14] This notion of utopia is not that of a separate, static place that fails to disturb the other element of a binary ('reality') to which it is linked, but rather a movement, a rhythm, a vibration, an instability, a becoming. Roland Barthes, as we have seen a key figure in Téchiné's development, in *Roland Barthes sur Roland Barthes* prefers the term 'atopia' for this reason, as precisely a movement which disturbs norms, the movement created by the utopia in a binary opposition to the doxa:

> Utopie (à la Fourier): celle d'un monde où il n'y aurait plus que des différences, en sorte que se différencier ne serait plus s'exclure... dès lors que l'alternative est refusée (dès lors que le paradigme est brouillé), l'utopie commence. Le sens et le sexe deviennent l'objet d'un jeu libre, au sein duquel les formes (polysémiques) et les pratiques (sensuelles),

13 'We are living at a time of significant sexual emancipation, and the work of repression is not necessarily a negative thing. I think that in a way what is liberated in one domain is crushed in another. There is always a swing of the pendulum.'

14 See also Marshall 1999–2000.

libérées de la prison binaire, vont se mettre en état d'expansion infinie. (Barthes 1975: 88, 136–137)[15]

As Téchiné told Barthes's biographer Louis-Jean Calvet on his 'non-coming out': 'Il voulait éviter deux pièges symétriques, la honte comme le triomphe' ('He wished to avoid two related traps, shame and triumph') (Calvet 1990: 218; 1994: 178).

Thus in Téchiné's pluralist narratives, homosexuality is one of the heterogeneous ways of being in the world, no more. In an interview accompanying the DVD edition of *Les Voleurs*, he adopts a vocabulary and a position which can be read as defending sexual pluralism against both heterosexist and gay militant interlocutors:[16]

> Des garçons attirés par des garçons aujourd'hui, ou des filles attirées par des filles, toute cette espèce comment dire de cloisonnement homo-hétéro, tout ça c'est un combat d'arrière-garde... Ce qui compte c'est la vie amoureuse des gens et là-dessus chaque personnage est minoritaire... Chaque personnage – comme chacun de nous dans la vie – est une minorité sexuelle à lui tout seul. (StudioCanal Video, 2004)[17]

This would sound like a rather traditional universalism – it does indeed make a difference in our culture whether one is (or acts) gay or straight (this is of course what Téchiné is denouncing) – if it were not for the creative use of 'minority' in his cinema. There we find gayness in 'minor' mode, but in being so it means that 'major'

---

15 'Utopia (à la Fourier): that of a world in which there would no longer be anything but differences, so that to be differentiated would no longer mean to be excluded ... Nonetheless, once the alternative is rejected (once the paradigm is blurred) utopia begins: meaning and sex become the object of a free play, at the heart of which the (polysemant) forms and the (sensual) practices, liberated from the binary prison, will achieve a state of infinite expansion': Barthes 1977: 85, 133. See also Bjørnerud 1992.

16 Radio F.G. (formerly Fréquence Gay) warned its listeners away from *Les Voleurs* as it was said to convey a negative image of lesbianism: Martel 1997.

17 'Today, boys attracted to other boys or girls attracted to other girls, all this kind of, what would you say, compartmentalisation, between gay and straight, that's all a rearguard battle ... What counts is people's love lives and there everyone is a minority ... Each character – like all of us in real life – is his or her own sexual minority.' Cf. Deleuze and Guattari: 'La sexualité est une production de mille sexes, qui sont autant de devenirs incontrôlables' (1980: 341); 'Sexuality is the production of a thousand sexes, which are so many uncontrollable becomings' (Deleuze and Guattari, 1988: 278).

positions, notably masculinity and heterosexuality, are relativised as well (Brassart 2000). So it is not that Gilles and Bernard in *Hôtel des Amériques*, or Jimmy in *Les Voleurs* (his highly sexualised scene with Juliette – he leaps naked out of bed to prevent her suicide and lies on top of her – is also marked by her observation that he never seems to have sex; he also gets on well with the transvestites at the night club) are 'really gay'. It is equally unhelpful to assert this of Pierre in *J'embrasse pas*, who does indeed have problems performing with women and, as his last visit makes clear, is more attracted to Romain than he admits. But the point about Pierre in the film is his *disavowal* of homosexuality as a possible constituent of his masculinity, and not homosexuality itself (a disavowal which in the case of his friend Saïd leads to violence).[18] Replying in 1991 to an interviewer from *Gai Pied Hebdo* who was rather disapproving of the film's 'timid' and 'negative' portrayal of homosexuality, Téchiné denied any self-censorship in his alteration of Nolot's original script (in which the plot revolved around pimps and Pierre discovering his 'real' homosexuality with Saïd):

> Ce ne sont pas les déclarations d'homo ou d'hétérosexualité qui me fascinent, mais, précisément, cette zone d'ambivalence très opaque, cette marge, cette lisière... Il y a autant de formes de sexualité que de personnes. Les schématisations ne servent, en dernière instance, que la bonne conscience hétérosexuelle. Introduire de l'homosexualité dans un contexte hétérosexuel me paraît plus 'dérangeant'.[19]

All these male characters partake, then, of a destabilisation of social and sexual assignments and positions. In *Ma Saison préférée*, there are sexual mysteries: in contrast with the predictably hormone-packed Lucien and the solidly dull Bruno, but with the same disconnectedness, Antoine is unmarried, unattached, a voyeur. Emilie has wordless anonymous sex with a handsome young doctor in a scene which could be a fantasy (it takes place along the same stretch of river in which she

18 In an interview, Téchiné declared that a different attitude by Pierre towards his homosexual possibilities would have needed to be treated in a wholly different film, and that the character of François in *Les Roseaux sauvages* enabled him to develop this: Jousse and Strauss 1994: 17.

19 'It's not declarations of homo- or heterosexuality which interest me, but rather that very opaque zone of ambivalence, the margin and border... There are as many forms of sexuality as there are individuals. Oversimplification just plays into the hands of heterosexual morality. Bringing homosexuality into a hetero-sexual context is much more "disruptive"': de Costa 1991.

converses as a child with her parents), or else a desperate succumbing to feeling – no matter what – in the context of visiting her dying mother (the seduction is forced, but on the second occasion she does not flee but simply sits on a bench nearby), a need on Téchiné's part to avoid the apparent desexualisation of at least one of the main characters, especially as this is the one thing she cannot and will not share with her brother. In any event, it is interesting to see Deneuve play a scene which more than anything else resembles an anonymous gay pick-up from films such as Patrice Chéreau's *L'Homme blessé* (1982) or Cyril Collard's *Les Nuits fauves* (1992).

Les Roseaux sauvages develops the idea of unfinished, aspirant becoming by portraying a group of teenagers doing the *baccalauréat*. For the first time since *Souvenirs d'en France*, Téchiné sets a film in the national past, in 1962 between the signing of the Evian accords in March and Algerian independence in July. (This final period of the Algerian drama was marked by the intensification of violence in France and especially Algeria by the OAS (Organisation de l'armée secrète), the terrorist group of European settlers (*pieds noirs*) and renegade French army officers, including General Salan, – his sentence to life imprisonment is mentioned in the film – who fought a rearguard scorched-earth battle to disrupt the independence process and perpetuate the polarisation between the European minority and Arab/Berber majority. The conflict ended in the summer with the mass exodus of *pieds noirs* from Algeria, which features on television newsreel in the film.) Whereas *Ma Saison préférée* had pluralised its characters temporally by bringing their pasts into the present, *Les Roseaux sauvages* makes of the past a continuous present, with a strong autobiographical element for Téchiné himself. The film was his first collaboration with co-scriptwriter Gilles Taurand since *Hôtel des Amériques*. In addition, this is his first film without stars, the young quartet at the centre of the film making among their first appearances on screen. Maïté (Elodie Bouchez), the daughter of Communist schoolteacher Mme Alvarez (Michèle Moretti) has a non-sexual friendship with François (Gaël Morel), who lives for literature and cinema and who has a one-night *branlette*/wank with fellow-boarder and peasant son Serge (Stéphane Rideau). It is the Algerian war which acts as catalyst for the transformations that follow. Serge's brother Pierre (Eric Kreikenmayer), who had asked Mme Alvarez to help him desert, is killed there by the OAS. An older student, Henri (Frédéric Gorny), is a repatriated and embittered *pied noir* with sympathies for the OAS (he originates from Philippeville in the Constantine region of Algeria, the scene of an infamous massacre by rebels of 123 French civilians in 1955; his father was killed in a bomb attack). Here there is a gay character discovering his sexuality, but this narrative is less important than its insertion into a certain historical moment, and into a network of construction and deconstruction of the imaginary edifices the characters have created for themselves, and which the older characters have bequeathed. The film's title refers to the poem 'Le Chêne et le roseau' ('The Oak and the Reed'), from the seventeenth-century fables of La Fontaine, and which François reads aloud from the blackboard in a literature class. In it, the reed proves over the oak the advantages of flexibility, as the tree is felled by a mighty wind. François is also attracted to Henri, whom Maïté calls a fascist. Henri is going to set alight the Communist Party headquarters but finds Maïté working there; she eventually overcomes her repulsion at his politics and responds to him sexually. However, there is no completion of the apprenticeship; the last embrace in the film is a chaste but passionate one between Maïté and François, this as they await their exam results while bathing in the river.

The first sound in the film is that of a man whistling over the credits a traditional Occitan love song, 'Se canto', the chorus of which is sung at the wedding and which Serge whistles in the final scene. The first conversation is about cinema, François attempting without success to persuade Maïté to go with him to see Ingmar Bergman's *Through a Glass Darkly* (1961), rather than go to Pierre's wedding. The south-west and cinema proclaim the strand of Téchiné autobiography. The wedding party sets the scene for, and sets in motion, the narratives of collective history and individual desire that the film successfully articulates. François's uptightness and distance from the community (contrasting with the exuberant and playful children in the scene) are established but not yet explained by his academic brilliance and uncertain sexuality; he is at first indifferent to his classmate, the handsome Serge, who asks Maïté to dance. Pierre reveals to Mme Alvarez that he married the first girl who said yes in order to get home leave, and implores her to help him. The wedding party is a classic Téchiné social scene, reminiscent of the final scenes of *Hôtel des Amériques*. Protagonists are situated socially, in time and space, and in relation to each other, but those relations are dynamic, not static. Through editing and a mobile camera, Téchiné conveys a shifting social whirl of alliances (the one element of fixity are François and Maïté sitting alone, slightly aloof, on the grass), tentative *rapprochements*, and separations (Pierre comes on too strong to Mme Alvarez and she leaves). The central conversation between the latter pair takes place as they dance to a waltz, their faces in close-up, moving in and out of frame as other figures, out of focus, move in front of and behind them. They are in the social whirl but this is also a capsule of anxiety and fear, indicative of a deeply troubled side to the community euphoria. The music they dance to is Johann Strauss' *Voices of Spring*, which was also used in the communion lunch scene in *Le Lieu du crime*: Lili's mother had put on some music 'to cheer us up' after an outburst of hatred from Thomas had disrupted the meal. The Strauss waltz is an ironic counterpoint as she encourages the adults to return to the table: it accompanies them as they are shot from behind as they sit down again, in silence, and the camera then circles them, ironically reproducing waltz-like movements. In the scene in *Les Roseaux sauvages*, the simultaneous reality of euphoria (not least because of the landscape, and this prefigures the final scene) and anguish is held in balance. Pierre turns off the music, but the protests from the guests fade into a spontaneous rendition of 'Se canto' – itself a lament for lost and distant love – which accompanies François, Maïté and Mme Alvarez as they are shot from behind walking back down the track. The next scene in the classroom introduces the 21-year-old Henri whose pro-French Algeria essay on Rimbaud meets with Mme Alvarez' disapproval. The story of François's awakening desire for Serge, and then Henri, is thus punctuated on the soundtrack with radio news bulletins from the deteriorating situation in Algiers.

Unlike, for example, the archetypal 'coming-out' narrative of André Gide's autobiography *Si le grain ne meurt*, François's story is not a teleological and euphoric one of discovery of a sexual 'self'. His fumbling exploration is a source of humour, as he worries to Maïté about his attraction first for Serge, then for Henri, and who knows what third person to come. His quest ends in some disappointment, as the shoe-shop owner, the only other 'gay in the village', it seems, proves kind but unhelpful in his request for advice, he is definitively rejected sexually by Serge in the closing scenes, his final embrace in the film being with Maïté (who has just lost her virginity to Henri, and parted from him). In contrast to his confession of an *act* to Maïté ('j'ai couché avec un garçon'/ 'I've slept with a boy'), the sheer effort of 'being gay' (or 'being' anything at all) is underlined in one of the film's central scenes, when, in an echo of rehearsals in front of a mirror from *Le Lieu du crime* and *J'embrasse pas*, he repeats to himself 'Je suis pédé' in the school bathroom. (Romain in *J'embrasse pas* had been made to pronounce the Deleuzean 'Aucun pédé ne peut dire, "je suis pédé"'/'No gay can say, "I am gay"'.) In a violent break from Téchiné's usual fluid camera, the scene is edited, after a narrow pan from François's face to that of his mirror image, into three jump cuts which progressively close in on him. As Emma Wilson points out, 'There seems a space between the words and his image, as there is between the face and its reflection' (Wilson 1999: 36). The final shot of him, of his two images, is that of a standard cinematic shot-reverse shot position, as his mirror-image is filmed above his left shoulder. This is also a break from Téchiné's standard practice of using two cameras, so that, for example, the conversation between François and Serge in the school toilets following Pierre's death is filmed with both boys clearly in shot.

As ever, identity in Téchiné is linked to provisionality and performance, and individual social, sexual and psychological positions are profoundly relational. The narrative chain of unreciprocated love – François for Serge/Henri, Serge for Maïté – reaches some kind of resolution in the final scenes, but is also important for the social and political pluralism, and dynamic interactions (or impasses) this generates. This is evident, for example, in a microcosmic scene when François and Henri, exempt from school sports, are watching the boys play rugby. As they eat from a food parcel of crêpes sent by François's parents (a reference to another space and time, the skeletal back story of François/[Téchiné]'s family),[20] François is of course watching Serge, who is stripped to the waist; the camera adopts his desiring point of view. There follows a shot of Henri in the same position, wearing his familiar dark, melancholic expression: the relationship between his mental world and the rugby field is distinct, in that the death of Serge's brother, and the earlier fist fight between the two boys, means the Algerian war is massively present even here. All this happens to the sound of Del Shannon's 'Runaway', a song denoting lost love, growing American pop influence in France, and the production requirement of including songs from the Polygram catalogue.

20 François's father is glimpsed once on his tractor, his (clueless) words to François and Maïté are then spoken off camera.

These remarks mean that the autobiographical dimension of *Les Roseaux sauvages* must also to an extent be pluralised. While François is clearly closest to the young Téchiné, Maïté's echo of Emilie's line in *Ma Saison préférée* describing her time at boarding school ('je ne fais qu'attendre'/'all I do is wait') seems also to speak from his own adolescent experience. Unlike, for example, Truffaut's 'autobiographical' *Les Quatre Cents Coups*, Téchiné's alter ego in *Les Roseaux sauvages* is one of four central characters, not to speak of the minor characters who move between foreground and background (particularly in this film the two schoolteachers, Mme Alvarez and her replacement Morelli, played by Jacques Nolot, with his agoraphobic Algerian wife Aïcha).

The remarkable 15-minute final sequence of *Les Roseaux sauvages*, one of the most memorable evocations of a natural scene in recent French cinema, in fact recapitulates many of the film's preoccupations with space and time. As André Gardies has pointed out, landscape in film is never simply 'there', but, because of the role of subjectivity and the spectator, tends to be the vector of connotative processes, as opposed to the denotation of 'places' (in *Les Roseaux sauvages*, Toulouse, Marseilles, Philippeville, and so on): 'Le paysage ne se réduit donc pas aux objets du monde répertoriés comme "paysages" mais s'ouvre aux configurations filmiques les plus diverses, jusqu'à permettre de parler, par exemple, de "paysage intérieur"'.[21] The sequence is soaked in narrative, as the protagonists' sexual longings set in motion by previous events are resolved: two of the three scenes with François and Serge alternate with the Maïté–Henri pairing. But we have seen in Téchiné the interrelation of physical and mental landscapes, and the presence of the virtual in the actual: the use of the 'ghost' of Pierre in Mme Alvarez's 'dream' sequence at the hospital is but one signal of this. Moreover, the sequence self-consciously draws on several intertexts. Leaves rustling in the breeze take us back to the beginnings of cinema and the wonderment caused by a similar sight in the background of, for example, the Lumières' 1895 film, *Feeding the Baby*. Two or three semi-distant figures within an abundant countryside recall impressionist paintings such as Claude

21 'Landscape is thus not to be reduced to an inventory of objects in the world called "landscapes" but opens out to the most diverse cinematic configurations, so that we can speak, for example, of "inner landscape"' (Gardies 1999: 148). See also in that volume François de la Bretèque's analysis of representations of the southern French landscape: de la Bretèque 1999.

Monet's 'Les Coquelicots'/'The Poppy Field' (1873) and Pierre-Auguste Renoir's 'Chemin montant dans les hautes herbes'/'Pathway through high grass' (1874). (The shot of François and Serge walking away from the camera on right of frame is very reminiscent of this.) And there is of course Jean Renoir's *Partie de campagne* of 1935, with which this sequence has often been compared. As in Renoir's film, a river is never just a river. The standard trope of flowing water connoting the passage of time is just the beginning of a complex evocation of time which we must first tackle, paradoxically, via notions of space.

One of the striking features of the sequence is the rigmarole involved in getting to this local beauty spot. For one thing, only Serge (and his late brother, who took girls there) seems to know about it, although it is not far from town, and François and Maïté are local too. So when the whole sequence is elegantly framed by the young people having to leap over a barbed-wire fence, denotations of 'place' do indeed seem to have been left behind. In the highly influential 1967 essay, 'Des espaces autres',[22] Michel Foucault writes of those spaces which do not quite fit into the contemporary regime of classifying and establishing relations between sites ('relations of proximity between points and elements'). These other spaces 'are something like counter-sites, a kind of effectively enacted utopia in which the real sites, all the other real sites that can be found within the culture, are simultaneously represented, contested, and inverted'. These 'heterotopias' in many ways hark back, in our desanctified world, to sacred spaces. Foucault even mentions the traditional honeymoon trip as based on the idea of a young woman's 'deflowering' taking place 'nowhere'. Heterotopias, which 'always presuppose a system of opening and closing', can also 'create a space of illusion that exposes every real space, all the sites inside of which human life is partitioned, as still more illusory'. Foucault's example at this point in his essay is that of the brothel, but we have seen how in Téchiné the partitions and classifications of modern life are always broken down.

This final sequence of *Les Roseaux sauvages*, dominated as it is by the river, is well prepared in the film. Its main – supremely temporal – connotation had been one of death as well as desire. Serge had bathed in a river, watched by Maïté, after he walked out of his brother's funeral (and he struggles to hide his erection). At one point

22 *Dits et écrits II* (Paris: Gallimard, 2001), pp. 1572–1573; Of Other Spaces, translated by J. Miskowiec, *Diacritics*, 16 (spring 1986), 22–27.

François encounters Serge on his way to drown a litter of cats in the river. But the crystalline reflectiveness of the water is also connoted by the abundance of mirrors and glass in the film, and of characters' images photographed simultaneously looking into and out of a mirror. Just before this sequence, François had finally plucked up the courage to speak with Cassagne, the gay shoe-shop owner. François is filmed, as in his first abortive visit, through the reflective panes of the shop window, and then the main part of the men's conversation is shot against a mirror: Cassagne's back is to the right of the frame, at an angle, his full image is seen gazing into (and out of) the mirror while François in the mirror looks up to him. Foucault is here worth quoting at length:

> I believe that between utopias and these quite other sites, these heterotopias, there might be a sort of mixed, joint experience, which would be the mirror. The mirror is, after all, a utopia, since it is a placeless place. In the mirror, I see myself there where I am not, in an unreal, virtual space that opens up behind the surface; I am over there, there where I am not, a sort of shadow that gives my own visibility to myself, that enables me to see myself there where I am absent: such is the utopia of the mirror. But it is also a heterotopia in so far as the mirror does exist in reality, where it exerts a sort of counteraction on the position that I occupy. From the standpoint of the mirror I discover my absence from the place where I am since I see myself over there. Starting from this gaze that is, as it were, directed toward me, from the ground of this virtual space that is on the other side of the glass, I come back toward myself; I begin again to direct my eyes toward myself and to reconstitute myself there where I am. The mirror functions as a heterotopia in this respect: it makes this place that I occupy at the moment when I look at myself in the glass at once absolutely real, connected with all the space that surrounds it, and absolutely unreal, since in order to be perceived it has to pass through this virtual point which is over there.

In Téchiné, mirrors offer opportunities for identity scrutiny, but rather than confirmation of identity they offer a non-fit, even if, as with François's earlier 'je suis pédé' scene, a character strains to fit. Rather, mirrors partake of an interchange of the real and the possible, the actual and the virtual.

This interchange is temporal as well as spatial, as becomes clear in the crystalline, heterotopic scenes from *Partie de campagne* and *Les Roseaux sauvages*. In the Renoir film, a middle-class family of shopkeepers go on an outing to the countryside near Paris. At an inn, the mother and daughter, who is to marry the father's rather boring employee, are first observed by two young local men through a window, who then attempt to seduce the two women, taking them on the river while their men fish and sleep. The encounter between the young Henriette (Sylvia Bataille) and one of the men is only partly consummated, but via a rainstorm sequence the action of the film moves forward in time to a new encounter between them, when she visits the same spot with her now husband. The sense of past time and of loss is overwhelming to them both. Here the river connotes not only the passing of time (and indeed death, at one point the young man is shot in the later sequence with a tree branch forming the shape of a guillotine and scaffold around his head). Its crystalline virtuality means that it also suggests different lives that might have been led, possible but incompatible timelines.

For Gilles Deleuze, in the crystal image we see time, in the sense of a double movement of presents that pass, but which also replace one another and move towards the future (Deleuze 1985/1988). In *Les Roseaux sauvages*, what we see in Renoir is complicated by the film's temporal stance. While it looks back on 1962 from a position thirty years later, and has a strong (but incomplete) autobiographical element, it manages paradoxically to conserve the familiar Téchiné tendency to suggest an open future. Although we know as spectators – or think we do – the destiny of François, we cannot know all that separates him from Téchiné the director in 1994; the fates of the other protagonists are unknown. The poem 'Le Chêne et le roseau', the youth of the protagonists, the suspension of time as they await their exam results, all conspire to reiterate the dual notion that the classifications of the adult world are determining factors in their make-up – hence the importance of putting them in a final heterotopic space – but that in the 'real world' they will not be determined by the past. Serge has already changed his mind about marrying his sister-in-law and remaining on the family farm. The last reaction shot is given to him, as he uncomprehendingly watches Maïté kiss François. What Wendy Everett calls 'the film's simultaneously retrospective and prospective regard' (Everett 1999: 54) is recapitulated by the shot that follows. A 360–degree pan photographs the natural scene, devoid of human figures, and ends on Maïté, Serge and François shot *from behind*. The 360–degree pan is a shot often associated with Renoir (the most famous example is probably from near the end of *Le Crime de Monsieur Lange*, also from 1935, in which it recapitulates the spatial and social relationships around the courtyard). Here in Téchiné the pan is temporal rather than spatial: the heterotopia of the final sequence does not lend itself to any kind of literal mapping, and in any case the central image of the river is absent from the panorama. Throughout the final sequence of the film, the forward motion of the narrative, helped by the crystal image of the water (and the fact the river is followed both up and downstream) has been accompanied by a laying down of memories. The tension between memory and loss is summarised in the last conversation between François and Serge: François, still reeling from Serge's definitive romantic rejection, declares he will never forget. Serge, having got over the death of his brother, declares that there is something worse than war itself, the fact that 'tout passe' ('everything passes'). The panoramic shot is valedictory, and therefore looks backward in time from the point of view of the present; but the shot of the three protagonists from behind, accompanied by optimistic whistling from Serge, means that they enter into a future we cannot as spectators fully know.

References

'Ciné Club', France Culture, broadcast 13 May 1998.

Barthes, R. (1975). *Roland Barthes*. Paris, Seuil.

Barthes, R. (1977). *Roland Barthes*, translated by R. Howard. London, Macmillan.

Bjørnerud, A. (1992). Outing Barthes: Barthes and the Quest(ion) of (a gay) Identity Politics. *New Formations*, 122–141.

Bonnet, J.-C. (1986). Enfances. *Cinématographe*, 118 (April), 20.

Brassart, A. (2000). Une Critique du modèle masculin: à propos des films d'André Téchiné, in D.Welzer-Lang (ed.), *Nouvelles approches des hommes et du masculin*. Toulouse: Presses universitaires du Mirail, 313–319.

Calvet, L.-J. (1990). *Roland Barthes 1915–1980*. Paris, Flammarion.

Calvet, L.-J (1994). *Roland Barthes: A Biography*, translated by S.Wykes. Cambridge, Polity Press.

de Baecque, A. (1993). Journal de voix et de bruits. *Cahiers du cinéma*, 467–678 (May), 36–43.

de Costa, E. (1991). Silence, on coupe! *Gai Pied Hebdo*, 494 (14 November), 56–59.

de La Bretèque, F. (1999). De Feuillade à Renoir: fonctionnalité, latinité et effets discursifs du paysage méditerranéen, in J. Mottet (ed.), *Les Paysages du cinéma*. Paris, Champ Vallon, 164–179.

Deleuze, G. (1985). *Cinéma 2: L'Image-Temps*. Paris, Minuit.

Deleuze, G. (1988) *Cinema 2: The Time-Image*, translated by H. Tomlinson and R. Galeta. London, Athlone Press.

Deleuze, G. and F. Guattari (1972). *L'Anti-Oedipe: capitalisme et schizophrénie*. Paris, Minuit;

Deleuze, G. and F. Guattari. (1975). *Kafka: pour une littérature mineure*. Paris, Minuit.

Deleuze, G. and F. Guattari (1980). *Mille plateaux: capitalisme et schizophrénie 2*. Paris, Minuit.

Deleuze, G. and F. Guattari (1984). *Anti-Oedipus: Capitalism and Schizophrenia*, translated by R. Hurley, M. Seem and H. Lane. London, Athlone Press.

Deleuze, G. and F. Guattari (1986). *Kafka: Toward a Minor Literature*, translated by D. Polan. Minneapolis, University of Minnesota Press.

Deleuze, G. and F. Guattari (1988). *A Thousand Plateaus: Capitalism and Schizophrenia*, translated by B.Massumi. London, Athlone Press.

Dubar, A. and J.-P. Joecker (1984). Entretien avec André Téchiné. *Masques: revue des homosexualités* (spring), 89–95.

Everett, W. (1999). Films at the Crossroads: *Les Roseaux sauvages* (Téchiné, 1994), in P.Powrie (ed.), *French Cinema in the 1990s: Continuity and Difference*. Oxford University Press, 141–152.

Foucault, M. (2001). Des espaces autres, in *Dits et écrits II*. Paris, Gallimard, 1572–5723.

Foucault, M. (1986). Of Other Spaces, translated by J. Miskowiec. *Diacritics*, 16 (spring), 22–27.

Freud, S. (1977). *On Sexuality: Three Essays on the Theory of Sexuality and Other Works*, translated by J. Strachey. Harmondsworth, Penguin.

Frodon, J.-M. (1993). Le 46ème festival de Cannes sélection officielle. *Ma saison préférée* d'André Téchiné. *Le Monde*, 15 May, 15.

Gardies, A. (1999). Le Paysage comme moment narratif, in J. Mottet (ed.), *Les Paysages du cinéma*. Paris, Champ Vallon, 141–153.

Hocquenghem, G. (1985). Où en est l'homosexualité en 85, ou pourquoi je ne veux pas être un 'écrivain gay'. *Masques: revue des homosexualités*, 25–26 (spring–summer), 111–113.

Hocquenghem, G. (1987). L'Homosexualité est-elle un vice guérissable? *Gai-Pied Hebdo*, 278–279 (11 August), 64–65.

Jones, K. (1997). *André Téchiné: la estrategía de la tensión*. Valladolid, Semana internacional de cine.

Jousse, T. and F. Strauss. (1994). Entretien avec André Téchiné. *Cahiers du cinéma*, 481 (June), 12–17.

Lalanne, J.-M. and D. Roth-Bettoni. (1994). *Les Roseaux sauvages*: André Téchiné, le Dépaysement. *Mensuel du cinéma*, 18 (June), 49–51.

Lardeau, Y. (1985). Flux d'amour. *Cahiers du cinéma*, 367 (January), 5–7.

Marshall, B. (1996). *Guy Hocquenghem*. London, Pluto Press.

Marshall, B. (1999–2000). Translation and Commentary on G. Hocquenghem, On Homo-Sex, *New Formations*, 39 (winter), 70–74 and 75–79.

Marshall, B. (2000). The National–Popular and Comparative Gay Identities: Cyril Collard's *Les Nuits fauves* (1992), in D. Alderson and L. Anderson (eds), *Territories of Desire in Queer Culture*. Manchester University Press, 84–95.

Martel, F. (1997). Dans la solitude des bibliothèques gay. *Le Monde*, 27 June, 1.

Nowell-Smith, G. (1987). Minnelli and Melodrama, in C. Gledhill (ed), *Home Is Where The Heart Is: Studies in Melodrama and the Women's Film*. London, British Film Institute, 70–74.

Sanders, V. (2004). *Sibling Love: The Brother–Sister Culture in Nineteenth-Century Literature From Austen to Woolf*. London, Palgrave.

Schuhl, J.-J. (2000). *Ingrid Caven*. Paris, Gallimard.

Taubin, A. (1996). Things Called Love. *Village Voice*, 23 April, 74.

Téchiné, A. (1996). Le Dépaysement humain (Interview). *Nouvelle Revue Française*, 520 (May), 41–57.

Téchiné, A. (2004). *Les Voleurs*. Interview. StudioCanal Video.

Wilson, E. (1999). *French Cinema since 1950: Personal Histories*. London, Duckworth.

4

Itineraries of Frenchness

In *Ma Saison préférée*, seemingly one of the most *intimiste* of his films, Téchiné deliberately opens out certain dialogues in spatial terms. Melding Bergmanesque emotional and interpersonal intensity with a characteristic emphasis on movement, he has key conversations take place at roadsides or at motorway service stations, cars roaring past. Furthermore, the film can also be read as a kind of primer on post-war French modernisation. The generational and spatial differences made explicit by distinct relationships to modernity also imply a national narrative: Antoine and Emilie's parents partook of developments in the 1950s when an older peasant rural France was transformed through mechanisation (the father formed a company making agricultural machinery), and an exodus from the land which propelled many, here their offspring, into urban and suburban settings and employment.[1] Moreover, the opening sounds of this film are in fact African, as Angélique Kidjo, from Benin, sings a traditional Tanzanian song, 'Malaika', over the credits. A Moroccan character, Rhadija (in fact played by Charlie Chaplin's granddaughter), plays an important contrastive role, coming from outside the family to disrupt their desires.

It is clear, then, that interrogations of Frenchness (a term preferable to the more prescriptive and static 'national identity') are a crucial part of the mix in Téchiné's explorations of modern life. But why *itineraries*? The examples from *Ma Saison préférée* already indicate Téchiné's aversion to investing identity in 'la France profonde',[2] and

1 For more on French 'modernisation', see for example Mendras 1988/1991; Ross 1995.
2 See the interview with Kent Jones: Jones 1997: 166.

this allows him a distinctive and ambivalent take on his native south-west. The emphasis in the films on movement dovetails with specific journeys, journeys moreover that are meaning-creating experiences. In his study of the origins of modern nationalism, Benedict Anderson has argued for the centrality of the journey in the creation of shared collective identities, in the religious pilgrimage, and then in the secular administrative apparatuses of absolutising monarchies in Europe (Anderson 1983: 55–57). In the abstract space of *Barocco*, journeys are aspired to but not achieved; in *Les Sœurs Brontë*, journeys are undertaken, boundaries are crossed. But the equivalent movements (or non-movements) in the films set in France, coupled with Téchiné's attentiveness to time and place, have quite different implications. Pierre's journeys in *J'embrasse pas*, developing that made by Nina in *Rendez-vous*, and Hélène and Gilles's aspirations to travel from Biarritz in *Hôtel des Amériques*, assert an idea of shared nation-hood while simultaneously interrogating the meanings of France and Frenchness. This is achieved by problematising the centre–periphery relation, by tackling Frenchness from marginal positions, by crossing boundaries, by 'making strange' and defamiliarising, in Brechtian manner in fact, any given, fixed, finished or 'natural' idea of the nation. These *plural* itineraries of Frenchness echo Téchiné's refusal when dealing with sexuality to alight upon stable 'gay' identities. Just as homosexuality serves to heterogenise the sexual, journeys and margins serve to heterogenise 'France'. Téchiné's films prompt the question, 'which France?' A word of which Téchiné is fond when describing his films is *dépaysement*,[3] whose literal meaning is that of being made to change country (*pays*), to be exiled, uprooted, lost, and thus in general to change place or milieu (significantly, in French this state of being – *dépaysement* – has both negative and positive connotations). For Téchiné, it is a kind of ontological category, describing the nature of human existence. In this chapter we shall examine its more literal dimension.

Alice et Martin (1998)

This can begin to be illustrated by looking at Téchiné's thirteenth feature film, *Alice et Martin*. In the south-west of France (these scenes

3 For example, the interview entitled 'Le Dépaysement humain': Téchiné 1996.

were shot in Cahors and Duravel in the Lot valley), Martin (as a child, played by Jeremy Kreikenmayer, as an adult by Alexis Loret) is the illegitimate offspring of an industrialist, Victor Sauvagnac (Pierre Maguelon) and a Spanish hairdresser, Jeanne (Carmen Maura). When Martin is 10 years old, Victor demands that he move into the Sauvagnac dynasty's home, and Jeanne agrees because of the opportunities she thinks this will bring. At the age of 20, Martin provokes the death of his tyrannical father when, threatening to leave, he pushes him down the stairs (a traumatic event fully narrated only two-thirds through the film, and a classic trope of melodrama if we recall staircase scenes from Sirk's *Written on the Wind* and even *Dynasty*). Briefly on the run in the countryside, Martin is released by the police when Victor's wife Lucie (Marthe Villalonga) covers up the real cause of death, whereupon he leaves for Paris to stay with his gay actor half-brother Benjamin (Mathieu Amalric), who shares an apartment with his close friend Alice (Juliette Binoche), a struggling violinist. Martin becomes a successful model in Paris, and after initial resistance on her part begins a love affair with Alice. However, Martin suffers a breakdown when, on a visit to Spain, Alice announces she is pregnant. Martin tells her the truth about his father's death, and indicates he can recover only if he pays for the crime. Alice travels to the south-west to a hostile reception from Martin's family, including his brother the mayor (Jean-Pierre Lorit). (Another brother, François (Eric Kreikenmayer), had been driven to suicide because of the firm's financial difficulties, his body discovered by Benjamin and Martin on the latter's twentieth birthday.). Alice meets with Jeanne and Lucie, and manages to persuade the latter to tell the truth to the police. Martin gives himself up to them.

After the critical and to an extent commercial success of his previous three films, Téchiné's career suffered a knock from the failure of *Alice et Martin. Cahiers du cinéma*, for example, historically so close to Téchiné's work, raised doubts about the viability of his narrative procedure. The reviewer criticised the linearity of the rather conventional flashback scene and the causality it implies, the incongruity of the epic sweep and the banal family narrative depicted (Faulkner – the character of Victor was inspired by that of Thomas Sutpen in *Absalom Absalom!* of 1936 – meets François Mauriac, the Catholic novelist of provincial bourgeois family secrets), and the hotchpotch of styles and treatments (Bouquet 1998). Indeed, the film is unusual in Téchiné's work for its extended depiction of a patriarch, here portrayed much more negatively than in *Souvenirs d'en France*, a film which shares the subject matter of a south-west industrial dynasty. This fact generates not only causality (the narrative's originary trauma), but also a pole of meaning, a homogenising or centripetal force which unusually defines Martin's quest for sanctification by the law, and which sits uneasily with the alternative emotional and sexual economies offered by Benjamin, Alice and Jeanne, an avoidance of filiation summarised by Benjamin as the alliance of 'le pédé et le bâtard' ('the gay and the bastard'). *Alice et Martin* is in some ways Téchiné-by-numbers: the south-west, the alternative bohemian family, the difficulties of Paris, the operations of money, the gay character, the pretty male lead, the quest for love in modernity, the child and the child within the adult. The much-heralded *retrouvailles* with Juliette Binoche are insufficient to carry the film. Although, as her work with Kieslowski and even Anthony Minghella has shown, she can play moral and spiritual depth, most notably due to the emotional range, subtlety and expressiveness of her beautiful and intelligent face, Alexis Loret is not her equivalent, although the film is actually about him. While he makes a brave stab at portraying Martin's emotional trajectory, he – and the rather conventional premise of the 'trauma' – are insufficient to merit the redemptive love bestowed on him by Alice. He is gorgeous rather than interesting, and that is one of the film's problems.

Nevertheless, there are many remarkable aspects to *Alice et Martin*, and the messiness of its overall edit is to some extent the flip side of the film's pluralism, which constantly tugs at, and even runs away from, the central narrative thread. That pluralism extends, for the first time since *Barocco*, to tangible pastiches or *hommages* to other directors, so that certain places and spaces in the film can be mapped according to (French) film history. Alice and Benjamin's life in Paris, the cramped flat, the marginal existence of young people, the constant movement, recall the *nouvelle vague* and in particular films by Godard (*Bande à part*, 1964; *Masculin/Féminin*, 1966). Indeed, the portrayal of the Paris fashion industry, with the proliferation of Martin's commodified image in advertising in the metro and elsewhere, are very Godardian.[4] Similarly, when Alice conducts her

4 Stéphane Bouquet (1998) likens the rapid cuts and use of shoulder-held camera in these sequences to the style of Olivier Assayas. See his portrayal of the rock-music milieu in *Désordre* (1986, starring Wadeck Stanczak), and of the life of

investigation of the provincial bourgeois milieu, we seem to be very much in the territory of murder enquiries to be found in films by Claude Chabrol. And Alice's final redemptive encounters with Martin recall the Catholicism of Robert Bresson, especially the final scene of *Pickpocket* (1959). However, Téchiné also demonstrates the distinctiveness of his approach. One striking aspect of Godard's (and others') 1960s films is the massive symbolic investment being made in the urban heterosexual couple, which, as Kristin Ross (1995) has argued, was part of a profound reordering of everyday life and individual identities which accompanied the process of modernisation. Téchiné's treatment, however, sidesteps the heterosexual couple in favour, at least temporarily, of alternative arrangements (though it must be said that Cédric Klapisch's *Chacun cherche son chat* of 1996 portrays a rather more convincing flatshare between a straight woman and a gay man). We shall also see that his specific treatment of provincial life, notably of course the south-west, is very distinct from Chabrol's generic portrayal of *'la province'*. For example, the latter's recent *La Demoiselle d'honneur* (2004) makes next to nothing of its setting in Nantes. Above all, Téchiné's distinctiveness lies in the combination and juxtaposition of different real (and cinematic) spaces, a pluralism which the itineraries within the film attempt to connect.

The prologue portraying Martin at 10 years of age ends with him, in winter, leaving the property by its iron gate, presumably for school, with Jeff Buckley's rendition of the melancholic 'Lilac Wine' on the soundtrack. The night before, he had stripped out of his pyjamas to stand naked in front of the open window as it snowed: deliberately to catch cold perhaps, as the father had seen through his ploy of pretending to have fever? To toughen himself against the new masculine regime of the father's house? In any case, he is photographed against a background, then foreground, of falling snowflakes, suggesting fragmentation, or perhaps a desire for indiscernibility. Ten years later, there follows a seven-minute sequence, largely devoid of language, of Martin on the run, and in transition. He rushes along the same avenue to open the same gate, three separate single bursts of strings on the soundtrack announcing drama. At this point, what follows is coloured by enigma, with the audience ignorant of what has transpired. There is a cut to his clothes strewn across grass, as the

contemporary Parisians in *Fin août début septembre* (1998). Certain sequences of *Alice et Martin* are also reminiscent of Robert Altman's *Prêt-à-porter* of 1994.

camera pans to a lake into which Martin slowly descends naked, the tranquillity of image and soundtrack then suddenly interrupted by him bursting to the surface, coughing and gasping for breath: he has chosen to live, or has attempted to be 'reborn'. The following scenes situate him outside of language, society, economy, family and nation, a would-be *enfant sauvage* who like Truffaut's character is yet to be acculturated, or who, because of trauma, aspires to be outside signi-fication. For the moment outside structures of commodity exchange, at night he 'gleans' food thrown out by supermarkets.[5] By day he treks through the countryside, Philippe Sarde's orchestral theme based on Bach's G Major suite for solo cello (also used in *J'embrasse pas*), and the vertical pans to mountain peaks, granting him a certain grandeur. Out of time and out of place, he wanders through deserted, off-season ski stations and chair lifts, finds a temporary shelter or 'home' in a shepherd's hut, the quest for fruit and eggs stolen from a nearby farm and chicken coop punctuated by encounters with carrion and its attendant birds of prey. He is finally cornered, terrified, in the coop by the farm's guard dogs, and, in the first words spoken in the sequence, the peasant couple hand him over to the police. Once more under the supervision and jurisdiction of the French state (much is made of the need for him to renew his identity card), his first words in the film as an adult are a surprised, 'je suis libre?' ('am I free to go?'): Lucie has vouched for him and is on her way. However, four shots then announce roads and lines of flight to follow: the first has him sitting on the ground near a bin outside a roadside service station as cars whizz by in the foreground. The camera then tracks him walking from right to left, behind a no entry sign (this motif recurs in a street scene in Paris), as a level crossing barrier closes (a shot reminiscent of that between Alex and Justin in *Les Voleurs*) and cars hurtle by in the foreground: he stretches out his thumb to hitch. He is then shot from behind as he faces the traffic, and a train crosses the frame diagonally from left to right. The next shot is of another train, a Paris metro on a overhead track crossing from left to right and framed in a window while a violin plays: the camera pulls back and we are in Alice and Benjamin's apartment. As the Paris sequence of the film begins, it is coloured by the ambivalences of this opening sequence: a 'rebirth' and a tabula rasa which are not quite complete, a set of potential

5 Agnès Varda's documentary *Les Glaneurs et la glaneuse/The Gleaners and I*, which explores this idea of 'gleaning', was released in 2000.

itineraries which lead in different directions (including potentially back from where he came), routes symbolically or mentally barred. At the same time, the 'silence', solitude and 'desert' of these seven minutes contrast dramatically with the tense, fast-moving, money-determined, aggressive social and spatial relations that prevail in the city, defamiliarising them, suggesting that the characters' emotional as well as physical itineraries will not end here.

The next significant journey in the film is to Spain, where Alice accompanies Martin to a photo-shoot in Granada. Although the Spanish connection is in part mandated by the film's co-production arrangements, it in fact generates three strands which act as counter-points to the film's central alienated spaces constituted by Paris and the provincial bourgeois family. The first is that of a popular immigrant culture in France itself, represented by Jeanne, played by the great Spanish film star Carmen Maura as a working-class heroine in slightly comic and hedonistic mode, damaged by Victor but free of the tormented interiority of the other characters. On the day of François's funeral, Martin meets up again with her former lover, the North African Saïd (Roschdy Zem). The second strand begins with a three-minute sequence in the Alhambra. Cutting from a shot of a disturbed Benjamin framed against his apartment window as a metro train passes by, the sequence begins with a slow tracking shot from left to right. For a split second Martin's right arm is glimpsed as the pair pass behind a pillar and the green and black mosaic which was used over the opening credits (to a song by the Breton multi-instru-mentalist Yann Tiersen, 'La Rupture', performed by Claire Pichet).[6] A tour guide is explaining in German the significance of this, the Mexuar Court, as Alice and Martin come fully into view and are then followed by the camera as they wend their way through the crowd of

6 Tiersen wrote the scores for *Le Fabuleux Destin d'Amélie Poulain* (Jean-Pierre Jeunet, 2001), and *Goodbye Lenin* (Wolfgang Becker, 2003). 'La Rupture''s appropriate lyrics, here sung in strangulated English, are as follows: 'Windows, doors, walls and carpets, chairs, tables and flowers, bread, wine,/butter and jam, fries, meat, beans and all spices/I've lost the taste of these things for two weeks now/I'm just waiting for a cup of dirty snow/airports, railroad stations, highways, streets and foggy lines/traffic, lights, cars and planes, boats, bicycles and walkers/now I'm wondering, blind, in the city/I'm surrounded by towers, made of dirty snow/faces, ears and bellies, backsides, legs, fingers and feet/ sweat, tears, dripping bodies, parties, someone is fucked up/now I'm quiet in this snow, snowy country/I'm hanging on until I am old, just older than now'.

tourists. The camera lingers on the central fountain, and then pans up as they admire the carvings and tiles of the south wall, continuing its trajectory to photograph the roof and blue sky. The first cut of the sequence moves from air to water, photographing the pair reflected upside down in a pool adjoining the Courtyard of the Lions; as it pans upwards, their conversation is about the secret of this place, what the architect was really thinking, something not provided in guide books. The third and final cut is to a tracking shot following them from left to right as they cross an inner room through a crowd listening to a guide in English, with light filtered through tiny window panes. Almost completely swallowed up by crowds which are now listening to a French guide, they circle and then enter the central space of Emperor Charles V's palace, built in classical style two hundred years after the rest of the Alhambra, where explanations are from a Spanish guide. Exiting the palace, Alice has a slight malaise and reveals her pregnancy to Martin; he faints when she asks him, 'Do you want to be a father?'.

The Alhambra sequence is to an extent another heterotopic space in Téchiné, both connected to and distinct from the other spaces of the film. The continuity with the mosaics of the opening credits points to a central thread, that of the relation between fragmentation and harmony. Martin is in pieces, he has been holding himself together through repression of a traumatic memory. The Alhambra illustrates the successful resolution in art of parts and whole, as well as the combination of air and water (the close-ups of the latter and the pans upward to the former echo in happier ways shots from the earlier sequence of Martin's *fugue*), and the embeddedness of different historical periods or pasts. It is also, of course, a supremely *dépaysant* space, a pinnacle of *European* Moslem culture, and the couple cross various languages in their walk through it. However, the news of the pregnancy provokes the return of the repressed, the return of home and *pays*, and Martin collapses.

After an interlude in a Spanish hospital, Alice and Martin construct another heterotopic space in an isolated beach house on the coast. Here Martin in particular attempts to construct a world abstracted from the rest, and in many ways the sequence again recalls the earlier *fugue* scene. Not only does Martin spend most of his time swimming, he, and to a lesser extent Alice, are often photographed as isolated figures in a landscape of rock and water. Their precarious financial situation also produces echoes of the earlier sequence, when Martin eats plums from a box of food brought by Alice, just as he stole from the farm. But his desperate aspiration to his own 'rebirth' collides with the realities of Alice's pregnancy and the crisis in their relationship: the long flashback to his twentieth birthday begins as he confesses his crime to Alice.

The final journey of the film is that of Alice to the south-west. Apart from the accents, and the landscape lovingly shot by Téchiné's director of photography Caroline Champetier in echoes of *Le Lieu du crime* (the river, a cemetery) and *Ma Saison préférée*, the main engagement with the cultural specificities of the region takes place at Alice's hotel. A rugby team is holding a party there, and, unable to sleep, she props up the bar with Saïd, who, however, is swallowed up by the partygoers as they dance and sing, stripped to the waist. A shot of three bare torsos, their arms entwined, is followed by one of Alice, fallen asleep. The homoerotic element, in contrast with Benjamin's gay life in Paris, is here disavowed in favour of a homosociality from which women are excluded. Otherwise, Alice's journey is a journey into the past, into Martin's past, and her 'love' is translated into a 'becoming-other', a 'becoming Martin': she is overwhelmed with emotion at the sight of the fateful staircase at the Sauvagnac home; the Jeff Buckley theme returns as she journeys through the countryside in Saïd's taxi; and she leafs through the same photographs of Martin's childhood that he had looked at on the day of his departure, and packed into his bag that Lucie had kept untouched after Victor's death.

Les Innocents (1987)

Les Roseaux sauvages was criticised in some circles for its political implications. Writing in *Le Monde*, Jean-Michel Frodon (1994) cast doubt on its false dichotomy, via La Fontaine, of rigidity versus suppleness, and for him the equally false symmetry of political intransigence (overcome by Henri and Maïté) and sexual prejudice (overcome or at least negotiated by François). *Cahiers du cinéma* pointed out the risk of rendering equivalent the Communist Party and the OAS (Jousse and Strauss 1994: 13). These criticisms seem to miss the point of the thirty-year gap between the events and the film. The explorations of personal and collective realities as lived by youth would have been

out of place amid the urgencies of 1962, in which political engage-
ments were unavoidable. Téchiné had long sought to make a film
about the Algerian War, and we have seen how even in the 1980s there
remained considerable obstacles to such an enterprise. Those who see
an absence of politics in Téchiné's later work might contemplate his
engagement with questions of immigration and racism. Even in 1975
and *Souvenirs d'en France*, he had problematised French identity by
making the dynasty a product of Spanish immigration. Serge in *Les
Roseaux sauvages* is of Italian stock. *Les Innocents* was made in 1987,
towards the end of a decade which had seen the electoral rise of the
Front national, a process that was to culminate in the presence at the
Presidential run-off in 2002 of its leader, Jean-Marie Le Pen. Téchiné,
along with his co-scriptwriter Pascal Bonitzer, produces in this film
what turned out to be a prescient analysis of racial politics in southern
France.

A young woman, Jeanne (Sandrine Bonnaire) arrives in a southern
French seaport (the unnamed Toulon) from northern France. It
is her first journey, and she has come to attend the wedding of her
older sister Maïté (Christine Paolini) to a North African, Nourredine
(Krimo Bouguetof), but especially to take back with her her deaf-mute
younger brother Alain (Stéphane Onfroy), with whom she had been
living following the death of their parents. Alain, however, has fallen
in with an Algerian man, Saïd (Abdel Kechiche, later to direct the 2005
César-winning *L'Esquive*), who had approached her on her arrival in
the city, and he runs off to be with him. Jeanne's first lead in looking
for the latter is the struggling orchestra conductor Klotz (Jean-Claude
Brialy), who knows and is indeed besotted by Saïd, but when she
visits his luxurious beach-side villa she encounters his son Stéphane
(Simon de la Brosse), who is recovering from a coma, and the latter's
overbearing mother Myriam (Tanya Lopert). Jeanne finds Alain and
moves into the modest hotel he shares with Saïd and which is run by a
repatriated *pied noir* from Algeria (Marthe Villalonga), and she begins
a sexual relationship with Stéphane, but there is a secret link between
the two men. By taking Jeanne to see a burns victim, Saïd reveals that
Stéphane had been part of a far-right racist gang which had set fire
to an immigrant hostel, and he had later been stabbed in revenge
by Saïd. During a brief stay in Algeria, Saïd telephones Stéphane to
tell him of the night he spent with Jeanne, and this motivates him
to denounce Saïd to the racist gang. However, Stéphane catches up

with him and warns him not to go back to the hotel, but Saïd drags him with him and they are both shot dead. The film ends with Jeanne staring at the two bodies.

In terms of realism, the filming of *Les Innocents* in Toulon turned out to be prophetic. Between 1995 and 2001 the town council was run by the Front national. Indeed, the far right found fertile terrain in a town in economic decline and marked by decades of municipal corruption, combined with remnants of Vichy ideology among certain retired navy men, Catholic–royalist sentiment among officers, militarism among officers at the arsenal, a clientele of small shopkeepers in the town centre, and OAS sympathies among the large *pied noir* population. Toulon is the only town in France to have a cenotaph dedicated to the martyrs of 'French Algeria', in a concession made by the long-serving (1959–1985) former 'republican' mayor Maurice Arreckx to the influential *pied noir* community (Rochu and Salhi 1996). However, this realist dimension is shadowed, as ever in Téchiné, by wider, and, in particular, mythical dimensions, signalled by the epigraph over the opening shot of the town: 'Once upon a time, in a city in the south of France...' unfolds after a tourist boat crosses the frame from left to right. The use of 'cité' in French as opposed to 'ville' connects with the extract from Sophocles' *Antigone* placed over the film's closing shot, which reproduces the first:

> CREON: Après le trépas les ennemis ne deviennent pas amis/Once an enemy, never a friend, even after death.
> ANTIGONE: Je m'associe pour aimer et non pas pour haïr/I was born to join in love, not hate. (Sophocles 1984: 86)

The Antigone story, in which the princess insists on burying her dead brother Polynices who was on the losing side of a war for the city of Thebes, an act which defies the social and political order prescribed by her uncle, King Creon, had of course been revived in France by the playwright Jean Anouilh during the Occupation in 1944. By invoking it here, Téchiné seems to wish to draw parallels with the divisions that persist in France in a post-war situation, that of the Algerian conflict, and to present in the figure of Jeanne a character who loves both the 'frères ennemis' Saïd and Stéphane beyond those political divisions (as Antigone also loved the dead Eteocles). While this is not the place to examine all the interpretations the myth has engendered, it is worth noting that the exploration of alternative sexual economies which Téchiné is fond of making in his films is echoed in the latest contribution to discussions of Antigone, Judith Butler's *Antigone's Claim*, which in a discussion of the relationship between kinship and statehood calls her –the daughter of Oedipus after all – 'not quite a queer heroine' (2000: 72). It is no exaggeration to claim, for example, that Antigone's love for Polynices is the fundamental brother–sister narrative in western civilisation. Notably, there is no equivalent in the film of Creon, no upholder of the Law, as both Klotz and the older far right gang leader are completely discredited as father figures.

The second intertext for *Les Innocents* is William Faulkner's *Light in August* (1932).[7] In that novel, a teenage woman, Lena Grove, arrives in a small town in the south of the United States (in fact she hitches there, just as Jeanne slightly bizarrely explains to Maïté that she took the train and hitched). Although the plot is very different from that of Téchiné's film, it similarly uses a young woman whose parents are dead as a catalyst for exposing the secrets, sexual and racial, of a community which is still dealing with the legacy of a past war, in this case the American Civil War. Some characters are completely weighed down by the past (the hotel owner in *Les Innocents*, who like Henri in *Les Roseaux sauvages* is from Philippeville – and is played by the actress Marthe Villalonga, herself a former *pied noir* – or the way in which, on a more personal level, Klotz obsesses about the errors of his youth); whereas both Lena and Jeanne live in the present. Jeanne to an extent gives Stéphane an apprenticeship of the present, and a new engagement in life: Téchiné, and the nervous, fragile performance of Simon de la Brosse,[8] work to contrast the beauty of the young man, often framed abstractly – and therefore freely – against the azure sea, with the demons that are tormenting him. However, Saïd provides Jeanne with an apprenticeship of the past, without which the present cannot be interpreted or life fully understood and embraced. The classifications of racism are of course the most insidious legacy of the past, and they work to destroy the marginal figures in both texts: the racially ambivalent Joe Christmas in *Light in August*; Saïd, who has no 'home' except the transitory hotel room, makes an unsuccessful first visit to Algeria and quickly returns, and who is associated with liminal spaces such as the airport pier and the beach (once he is shot walking

7 Acknowledged for example by Pascal Bonitzer in a radio interview: 'Ciné Club', France Culture, 13 May 1998.

8 Simon de la Brosse committed suicide in 1998 at the age of 33.

exactly at the frontier where waves and sand meet); and Stéphane, emotionally damaged by his upbringing, confused and unsettled in relation both to the hyperbolic idea of 'France' associated with the far right and to the multiracial reality of the town outside the semi-fortified family home.

The modernist melodramas associated with the Faulknerian tradition meld together of course questions of sexual desire and race. Joe Christmas ends up being not only shot but castrated. In *Les Innocents*, Téchiné's homoeroticism allows him to develop a masculine but not homosocial melodrama, across emotionally and physically fragile (Stéphane) masculine bodies, and around the pivotal figure of Saïd, object of desire for all the main characters: the despairing and alcoholic Klotz, Jeanne, and also in fact Stéphane. The scene in which Saïd and Stéphane meet for the first time in the film is one of the most remarkable in the whole of Téchiné's work. Saïd had visited the infatuated Klotz and asked for money so he could return to Algeria. As he leaves, Jeanne and Stéphane arrive, as Jeanne is looking for Alain, and Klotz is thus far, she believes, her only link to Saïd. Klotz is rehearsing a piece (a Philippe Sarde composition based on an eighteenth-century theme) with his orchestra. The confrontation between the two young men takes place to music, amid the empty theatre seats, and largely in silhouette. As the camera pans leftwards from Klotz and the orchestra, it frames Saïd against the dimly lit, slightly golden seat rows. He walks up the steps, and an editing cut shifts 90 degrees and films him from above, moving from right to left. Another cut shows Jeanne and Stéphane moving diagonally from right to left down the opposite steps. These shots alternate until Stéphane stops in his tracks. (Téchiné's cinematographer Renato Berta has compared this inevitable confrontation to that found in a western; Philippon 1988: 137.) Another shot shows both figures from the position of the stage, on a diagonal line from bottom left to top right, separated by the seat rows. Closer shots follow a shot-reverse-shot pattern as the figures slowly move towards each other; Jeanne and Stéphane are tracked from right to left in silhouette until they reach Saïd. The camera then moves 180 degrees to view them from the opposite direction, with the stage, orchestra, and starry backdrop in the background, the stars connoting particles, choreographies, arrangements in constellations and destiny. Returning to the previous camera position, Saïd breaks the immobility and is tracked left to right, while Jeanne follows him and utters the first words of the sequence, asking about the where-abouts of Alain. Saïd, for whom this is the last thing on his mind, swiftly replies, 'chez moi', and moves off. Jeanne returns to Stéphane to say she has to go, and then, after the camera switches 180 degrees again, he is alone to left of frame, his father with his back to him as he continues to conduct. As Stéphane turns to face him, he has a seizure, and, as Jeanne and Saïd turn back, he is photographed against the background of seats, staggering, landing on the ground with a thump that stops the music, which is now replaced by the sound of Jeanne's feet as she rushes down the steps towards him, and the sound of the musicians standing up and walking to the front of the stage to watch what is happening.

It is rare in cinema, or even in twentieth-century western culture (though not earlier) for there to be a representation of a man collapsing with emotion. The unusual *mise-en-scène* summarises the complexity of Téchiné's procedure: the heterogeneous juxtaposition of (still secret) violence and classical music, and which, along with the intri-cate choreography, contributes to the interplay of form and emotion; and the fluidity of private and public, as the personal drama between the two men (and, by extension, the narratives of Jeanne and Klotz), are played out in the open, with a real audience (the musicians), and a virtual one (the empty seats standing in for a missing collectivity, the cinema audience, the city, the nation). This not only implies that the drama involves wider, collective issues, it also suggests a revers-ibility of performer and spectator, and an understanding of the perfor-mativity of identities and boundaries. This is confirmed by the later appearance of the singer Marie-France (her first in a Téchiné film since *Barocco*) in a nightclub scene with Jeanne and Stéphane in the audience, in a rather camp rendition of 'Prends-moi'.

One possible criticism that can be made against *Les Innocents* is that Jeanne's role as a catalyst results in her in fact remaining on the margins of what is ultimately a boys' story (Jones 1997: 105–6). The film's pluralism does not extend to her inhabiting or exploring alter-native female spaces, unlike those created in *Les Voleurs*: her relation-ships with Maïté, Myriam, and the hotel proprietress are very limited. However, there are important scenes in which she enjoys autonomy and development in the film. The 'catalyst' is distinctly feminine, her gender makes a difference, in that she is to be located outside the games, pitfalls and disavowals that characterise the world of the men and which lead to their self-destruction.

When Jeanne encounters Saïd for the first time in the street, the gaze upon her is neutral: first shot from behind, he is watching her but there is no point of view shot from him. The sequence that follows is that of Maïté's wedding party, located in a courtyard that is both a typical Téchiné 'other space' and a rich evocation of North African culture within the boundaries of France itself. Jeanne is filmed descending steps into it, and then without an editing cut the camera follows her concerned and mystified look, tracking leftwards, a whitewashed wall momentarily filling the frame and acting as a boundary. Then in long shot it films an array of colour, movement and music. Maïté, at first hidden behind trees, literally emerges to greet her, and after introducing her initially cold husband, accompanies Jeanne so that she can change into an appropriate dress. This time an editing cut has them walking behind the same trees: Jeanne seems to have been absorbed into the space, one that is in fact not static, but characterised by change, as Noureddine is refitting the communal house.

However, this complex ten-minute sequence is both Renoiresque in its use of a mobile camera to establish in spatial terms community and social relationships (including the segregation of men and women, as crane shots on two occasions enable camera movement from one group to the other), and also intensively narrative. The first crane shot moves over the heads of the men in the foreground, to the women, and then pans leftwards along open windows to one that is closed: the shutters are opened by Alain. Jeanne, momentarily carried away by the music and dancing in the North African red dress Maïté offered her, then spies him, and the camera follows her as she ascends the stairs, from which she reappears to embrace Alain (this is virtually a quotation from *Le Crime de Monsieur Lange*). This movement is repeated in a night sequence, as Noureddine sings with the men, the camera moves over to the female group, and then up to Alain's closed window. Narrative is also generated by movement, as, in a manner typical of Téchiné, new relations are established within the social whirl. Jeanne meets Klotz, who launches a new narrative enigma by explaining that he should never have brought Alain back, and also anticipates the film's denouement by quoting the Koran on destiny. The sequence is also full of editing, establishing divisions between inside and outside, and establishing 'private' zones in which difference from the community, represented by the figure of Klotz (who transgresses the gender boundaries of the party), is further developed, and embodied, by Alain, soon to be joined by Jeanne.

Jeanne therefore, as much as anyone in the film, is to be understood as living the same dilemmas of belonging and departure, inside and outside, location and aspiration, connection and escape (White 1995: 75). Not only is the courtyard wedding party and community to be understood as 'un-familiar' and surprising in relation to the 'France' she had known outside, its complexity will emerge from that other space to affect her understanding of the city and nation beyond. Maïté is seeing other men as well as her husband. Alain aspires to the other place represented by Saïd's photographs of empty Algerian desert landscapes, and he physically prevents Jeanne from tearing them from the wall. He has to be rescued as he attempts to swim out to sea to join Saïd in North Africa. But Jeanne also, momentarily, drops out of the narrative, buying a yellow dress, changing her hairstyle, and becoming a *flâneuse*, wandering the city streets eating a sandwich. To Stéphane's disapproval, she replies, 'C'est comme si ce n'était pas moi, c'est plus marrant' ('It's as if it wasn't me, it's more fun').

As the film races to the tragic denouement, Stéphane pursues Saïd to warn him not to return to the hotel, but he initially takes this as jealousy of his relationship with Jeanne. Novelistic strands are reiterated as they pass through an open-air *bal* in which locals are dancing a waltz. Mythical and cosmic dimensions are invoked as Jeanne watches on television footage of an erupting volcano, and the hotel dog whimpers in anticipation of catastrophe. Saïd drags Stéphane into a suicide pact, 'like brothers', when he learns he has denounced him. As they turn a corner, three shots ring out which coincide with three jump cuts (unusual in Téchiné, repeated only in the violent 'je suis pédé' identity desperation of *Les Roseaux sauvages*) of the same empty scene. Jeanne rushes down the street, but here Téchiné suddenly changes light to dark (the same technique is used when Alice views the fateful staircase in *Alice et Martin*), reproducing the dual inner and outer, psychological and social character of the event. Stéphane is still alive, but despite his protestations he will not this time wake up from a long sleep. The two young men are, in death, almost physically entwined: Téchiné photographs their faces side by side, in an ending which recalls that of *Romeo and Juliet*.

Loin (2001)

Téchiné often states that he makes every film against the previous one. After the relatively big-budget star vehicle *Alice et Martin*, and its lack of success, he was in fact obliged to do so. *Loin* had only a limited international distribution, largely perhaps because of the absence of stars. Shot on digital video for budgetary reasons, the film was eventually financed mostly by UGC through the producer Saïd Ben Saïd, at a relatively modest cost of 24 million francs (£2.4 million).[9] *Loin* is almost entirely set in Tangiers, and to an extent revisits some of the territory of *Les Innocents*. Here, however, the liminality of a southern French port is replaced, extended, by a portrayal of the border of Europe rather than of the nation-state. *Loin* tells the story, over three days, of three central characters and, typically, a host of secondary figures who nonetheless have their moments in the foreground and who give social shape and texture to the film. Serge (Stéphane Rideau) is a 25-year-old French lorry driver who regularly transports clothes back and forth between Europe and Morocco and who is tempted by illegal trafficking. He is in an on–off sexual relationship with Sarah (Lubna Azabal), a Moroccan Jew who runs a guest house in Tangiers, and who on the death of her mother has to decide whether to stay or to be with her successful businessman brother in Montreal. Saïd (Mohamed Hamaidi) is a young Moroccan who dreams of escaping to Europe, eventually persuading Serge to smuggle him in his lorry to Spain. There is also Emily (played by the playwright Yasmina Reza, whom Téchiné met on the jury at Cannes in 1999), Sarah's sister-in-law, a novelist who has recently lost her son; James (Jack Taylor), a now elderly American gay man who has lived in Tangiers for decades; François (Gaël Morel), a French filmmaker who, in a reference to *Les Roseaux sauvages*, went to school with Serge in the south-west; and Farida (Nabila Baraka), an optician, separated from her husband, and who gives birth during the film.

This mobile and disparate material is held together, and is in relation with, a structure of time (three days), and of characters (three main whose names begin with 'S', French, Arab and Jew), all of whom are associated with different modes of transport: Serge's lorry, technologically advanced, standing out in its red colour, the nearest to 'home'

9 For an insight into the gestation of *Loin* and the complex production arrangements, see Frodon 2000.

Serge seems to possess; Sarah's motor scooter, its front headlight picked out in the night, shot from the front, following a conversation with Farida about stars; Saïd's bicycle, which he constantly pedals even when stationary, and which he despairingly loses in a confrontation with a money-changer.

The most significant structuring pole is of course the frontier, the strait of Gibraltar, the passage of goods, the boundary between East and West, First World and Third. Four points may be delineated which speak to the multiple connotations of the border. Borders are of course inside as well as outside, and it is Slavoj Žižek's argument in *For They Know Not What They Do* that borders, margins and peripheries are in fact an inherent part of what we take identity to be. Identities are always about non-identity, a split between what for example a nation, is, and what it purports or 'ought' to be, that totalisation or plenitude which can never by definition be achieved or grasped. The *boundaries* of national identification have to be understood as being reflected in the nation's internal *limits*, the impossibility of being fully, purely and unproblematically French (or European, or Moroccan): 'every boundary proves itself a limit: apropos of every identity, we are sooner or later bound to experience how its condition of possibility ... is simultaneously its condition of impossibility' (Žižek 1991: 110).

Furthermore, this lack at the heart of identity introduces the idea of a minor culture in the sense given that word by Deleuze and Guattari. This refers not to 'minorities' as such, but to 'des germes, des cristaux de devenir, qui ne valent qu'en déclenchant des mouvements incontrôlables et des déterritorialisations de la moyenne ou de la majorité' (Deleuze and Guattari 1980: 134).[10] In other words, as we saw in the previous chapter concerning gay sexuality, 'minor' identities, positions, becomings, generate new forms and practices, and, rather than building new plenitudes and fixities, undermine a major culture's claims to the natural and dominant. It is in this way that 'Frenchness' can be questioned, interrogated, even reinvented, from the margins and peripheries.

Third, borders – of nations but also of the self – are fundamentally performative, in the sense that Judith Butler (1990) draws on to talk about gender identity: language use which enacts a new reality as in 'I

10 'seeds, crystals of becoming whose value is to trigger uncontrollable movements and deterritorializations of the mean or majority', Deleuze and Guattari 1988: 106.

pronounce you man and wife', or 'the territory between that point and that point is ours'. Identity is thus no more than a stylised repetition, although no less real for that. This reference to gender is germane to Téchiné's wider procedure: there are parallels to be found in his treatment of same-sex relations (which do not alight upon a stable notion of gay identity), and of nationhood. In both cases his strategy is, through a process of *dépaysement*, to introduce heterogeneous elements into the doxa, be it one of hetero-normativity or nationalism, Parisianism, regionalism, here Eurocentrism.

Fourth, that performativity is attached to histories of power and discourse, so that identity is also a material practice (fences, customs posts). In this way the questions of identity in *Loin* are of course bound up with colonialism, post-colonialism, globalisation and Orientalism, that Eurocentric discursive figuring of the non-western other.

Téchiné's film *Loin* tackles these issues in its narrative composition and in its *mise-en-scène*. It fits with difficulty into an account of 'French national cinema', as, although it is written and directed by a Frenchman, it is co-written with the Moroccan writer Faouzi Bensaïdi (who appears in the film as Serge's contact in Algeciras) and is moreover quadrilingual, with dialogue in French, English, Spanish and Arabic, as well as a prayer in Hebrew. (Indeed, as in Renoir's *La Grande Illusion*, another film about the performativity of identity and borders, the main protagonist's inability to speak a language – in this case Arabic – contributes to his disempowerment, a fact not lost on the audience due to subtitling.) At the same time, in somewhat more documentary mode than Téchiné's other films, it continues his style of Balzacian realism, in which modernity is dissected via a painstaking emphasis on money (physically, as for example when Saïd counts out his savings), exchange and circulation (the details of the customs inspection, the contact explaining that he is just 'un maillon de la chaîne'/'a link in the chain' and doesn't even know who he works for), and the juxtaposition of different historical strata, the traditional and the modern (Emily's first act is to go to an internet café and send an email to Australia, one of Serge's meetings with a member of the smuggling network is in McDonald's, Sarah and Serge's employer Nezha (Rachida Brakni) playfully use wipes from different international airlines).

This minorising approach to identity via margins and frontiers is achieved via several characteristics typical of Téchiné's filmmaking procedure. The first is that of movement, which helps to ensure that Tangiers does not freeze into a Eurocentric myth typical of its representations in, say, Hollywood 'B' movies (*Flight to Tangier*, Paramount/director Charles Warren, 1953; *Tangier Incident*, Monogram/director Lew Landers, 1953) or even Bernardo Bertolucci (*The Sheltering Sky*, 1990). The DVD camera, while not dramatically lighter in weight than 35mm, nonetheless allowed Téchiné to operate with a smaller team (in fact himself, his cinematographer Germain Desmoulins on second camera, and a continuity girl) that was able to penetrate the urban streets and film in the thick of crowds. While the technology did not enable the dolly or crane shots to be found in other Téchiné films, the characters, poised between uncertain futures, are either filmed in movement themselves, as we have seen, or are shot as movement goes on around them: Serge and Saïd interrupt a dance class when they arrive at James' house, Serge and Sarah meet for the first time in the film as a goods train passes behind them, they later cross waste ground on which hordes of young Moroccans are playing, Sarah and François sit on the beach surrounded by acrobats – in fact Saïd's former profession – and then walk through them to the sea). It is this ability to see the characters as particles as well as persons which means that the social and psychological are seamlessly interwoven. One beautiful example is the cut from a star-filled night sky (seen through Farida's telescope) to the single headlight of Sarah's scooter filmed from in front as she returns home, Juliette Garrigues's score on cello momentarily blocking out any diegetic sound. Téchiné creates social but also mental worlds, in which emotional states befitting the melodrama or love story are articulated, via point of view shots, with the landscape. Serge's looking out to sea on the ferry as he travels to Morocco, Saïd gazing at Spain from a favourite vantage point in Tangiers, are examples of this. A more extended example is that of Sarah glimpsing a snake as Serge dozes on her lap, an image with multiple connotations that both speak to her mental state – of danger, anxiety, punishment, a fall – and echo elsewhere in the film: the little boy killed by a cobra in Renoir's *The River* (1951) that almost alarms Emily away from seeing the film that François is presenting at the cinematheque, the image of Saïd crawling on his belly beneath Serge's lorry at the end. This interplay between particle and person, social and psychological, movement and identity, implies that while society and history are determinants, they are never wholly determining, and that there are always spaces in-between, new becomings to be had.

This is true of the two main identity issues the film addresses, namely gender and sexuality, and East–West (although, given the materialism of its analysis, it is no surprise that class is an important issue between Serge and François, and to an extent Serge and Sarah). Two shots from Serge's point of view, and his reaction, are here worthy of comment. One is towards the contact he meets at the Tangiers bus station, and who interrupts the conversation to spread out a rug to pray. Another is towards a European lorry driver saying goodbye to a Moroccan woman and child at the port (and who later seems to be involved with traffickers). The reaction to cultural difference in the first example is partly qualified by the procedure in the second, in that it is the virtual which is in play for Serge, rather like the gazes out to sea, or Sarah looking at a picture book of Canada. These are gazes towards possible worlds and not towards absolute otherness. In any case, one of Serge's very 'French' habits, dipping his *tartine* into coffee, becomes the source of some bemusement for Saïd.

Apart from Saïd, it is overwhelmingly Moroccan women, not men, who articulate the social contradictions of their existence. A world of women is filmed across a variety of roles and spaces – maternal, sexual, in domestic and in paid work. There is no Oedipal trajectory in the film, a stable heterosexual couple is not formed, the male protagonist's action narrative comes to nothing, although a male friendship is reconciled. Indeed, one of the few couples referred to in the film is, jokingly, that old one formed by Farida and James. An alternative, extended family is momentarily portrayed at Farida's lunch party when she has to be rushed to hospital and – metonymically when we consider the rest of the film – the car at first won't start (although this is not *Le Quai des brumes*: escape and movement take place and fatality is avoided). Saïd professes no interest in sex with either gender, even as François attempts a half-hearted seduction of him. He thus avoids one European sexual myth of North Africa, even as François, intending to move to Tangiers, seems to wish to perpetuate it. (The film in fact very much pluralises its spectacle of the body across the three attractive main protagonists.) The mythic role of Tangiers in western literature – via Paul Bowles or William S. Burroughs – is addressed via the American character James, whose dialogue is lifted from a local newspaper interview with Bowles himself. He is accused by the women of associating Morocco with past and tradition: 'Il nous en veut d'être sorti de la préhistoire' ('He hates us for leaving the Stone Age').

Téchiné in an interview described Tangiers as one of those 'espaces-frontières, les lieux qui sont à la fois ponts et barrières, les lieux de passage' ('frontier-spaces, places that are both bridges and barriers, places of transit') (Kaganski 2001). Téchiné's mobile and minor cinema undercuts the fixity of myth, whether of Europe, North Africa or identity in general. It recognises the play of external borders and internal boundaries while aspiring to overcome them with the realisation that the other is contained within the same and vice versa: 'Il y avait l'idée du bord, de la bordure, de ce qui est le plus lointain dans le proche, ou le plus proche dans le lointain'. ('There was the idea of the edge, the border, of what is the most distant in the most close, or the most close in the most distant') (Kaganski 2001). This of course translates in Tangiers into an overcoming of the binary oppositions prevalent in Orientalism, with the city as 'l'Orient de l'Occident et l'Occident de l'Orient' ('the East of the West and the West of the East') (Guichard 2001: 24).

In this context it is interesting to consider the reason for the inclusion of *The River*. Téchiné was no doubt very conscious of this precedent in French cinema of an auteur making a film in an 'exotic', formerly colonised location. Renoir's film is famous for its evocation of the eternal rhythms of time represented by the Ganges, and its spiritual and universal ambitions in its sensual and luminous portrayal of the Indian landscape. Needless to say, the film has been taken apart in post-colonial readings, most notably for the evacuation of history and politics from this story of an English colonial family (Bhatia 1996). The clip which is shown in *Loin* is from the opening, as a traditional painting of rice and water is drawn in the sand as a sign of welcome, and the narrator (June Hillman) announces that this is a story of first love: 'First love must be the same any place ... but the flavour of my story would have been different in each'. While Téchiné is a firm admirer, and at times a disciple, of Renoir, and is not himself averse to a certain universalism, it is possible to argue that here *The River* represents a problematic, a source of debate (which is precisely what it is going to be at the Tangiers *cinémathèque* screening) rather than a master text. The questions are posed by this opening sequence: how is a European filmmaker to make a film in such a location? What is the relation of universal and particular? This reading is all the more appropriate in that, although François in *Les Roseaux sauvages* was a kind of alter ego for Téchiné, and is in Tangiers to make a film about illegal immigration to Europe, he is not exactly a reliable source of truth and evaluation in the film, and risks becoming a new James, entranced more than anything by Morocco's sexual possibilities. As we have seen, *Loin* works very hard to deconstruct the Eurocentric gaze.

The climactic scene of *Loin* is that of Saïd's escape, taking place in that contemporary emblem of margin, periphery and border, the no man's land of the ferry port where goods circulate more freely than people. The sequence lasts eight minutes, the first half of which is without dialogue, reminiscent of the Bressonian attempted car theft sequence in *Les Voleurs*, as Saïd makes it into the port area and gets to Serge's lorry in a montage of close-ups of his terrified face, shots from his point of view often filmed from a low angle as he crawls under vehicles, tracking shots, entry in and out of frame, and at one point a shoulder-held shot in front of him. These procedures reiterate much of what has gone before, in terms both of specific scenes (Saïd's gymnastics in climbing a wall recall the beach acrobats and also the young boys, watched by the women, exercising on rings, and Saïd had earlier inspected the underneath of Serge's lorry) and also narrative structure: a view of the sea; the snake, Serge's winding passage as he drives through the mountains, and now Saïd's movement echoing the sinuousness of the narrative; his ploy of (surreptitiously) joining a group of persons and then darting away, like a particle colliding, or the groups of individuals in the film joining together then parting. Even more remarkably, the sequence would make sense even without the images, as the soundtrack progresses from the conversational murmur of the scores of other would-be clandestines gathered near the port, through the sound of the sea and ship's horn which gives Saïd encouragement, and then of him sliding down walls, crawling on the ground, and of his footsteps on the tarmac. This part of the sequence ends with the sound of lorries starting, conversations overheard, and finally Serge's keys jangling. There is a brief return to 'normal' narrative, as Serge sees other clandestines being caught and conducts another check of his lorry, revealing Saïd hiding under the chassis. In a variation on shot/reverse shot, he tells Saïd when to rush into the cabin. Then the filming style shifts again, to a point of view from the driver's cabin, the lorry waved by police on to the ship. Angélique Kidjo singing 'Sene' now completely replaces the diegetic sound until the end of the film, except for the sound of a ship's horn and of waves over an image of the ferry as seen from the shore. As with Sarah's scooter ride, the dominance of non-diegetic music signals mental landscapes, emotional consequences, interiorities. And by using the same Angélique Kidjo track that accompanied Serge at the beginning of the film as he crossed the Straits of Gibraltar, and when he was on the road in Morocco itself during the central abortive involvement in trafficking, Téchiné not only creates a structural unity, he creates a privileged moment shared between the two men, while at the same time indicating that this 'ending' – the song ends very abruptly, and cuts off the final image – is in fact, for both of them, just part of a longer road.

Les Egarés (2003)

Téchiné's next film, *Les Egarés*, is unusual in his *œuvre* for several reasons. Like *Les Sœurs Brontë* and *Les Roseaux sauvages*, it is set in the past, and, like the latter film, in the national French past. It was also a commissioned work, by its producer, Jean-Pierre Ramsay Levi of FIT productions (which had also produced Claude Chabrol's 1993 documentary *L'Œil de Vichy* based on collaborationist newsreels and using the same historical advisor as *Les Egarés*, the historian Jean-Pierre Azéma). *Les Egarés* was also Téchiné's first literary adaptation, the script, which he co-wrote with his long-time collaborator Gilles Taurand, being based on Gilles Perrault's 2001 novella, *Le Garçon aux yeux gris*.[11]

Set between 10 June 1940 and the period just following the armistice signed between Hitler and Marshal Pétain on 22 June which established the Vichy regime, *Les Egarés* tells the story of a middle-class schoolteacher from Paris, Odile (Emmanuelle Béart), whose husband had been killed at the beginning of the war. Along with thousands of other refugees heading south of the capital, she is driving with her two children, 13-year-old son Philippe (Grégoire Leprince-Ringuet)

---

11 Perrault 2001. The following year Perrault published a sequel, *La Jeune Femme triste*, which recounts a return to the house by the older Cathy ('Sylvie' in the novella).

and 6-year-old daughter Cathy (Clémence Mayer). When the refugees are strafed by German planes, their car is destroyed, and they flee into woods with a mysterious 17-year-old stranger, Yvan (Gaspard Ulliel). They end up in an isolated, abandoned house where for a time they constitute an alternative family. Briefly interrupted by two soldiers from the defeated French army (Samuel Labarthe and Jean Fornerod), the idyll then comes to an end with the arrival of the police, but not before Odile and Yvan have sex. In a refugee centre, Odile learns that Yvan's real name was Jean and he had escaped from a reformatory; he has hanged himself in custody.

Despite the distinctiveness, including the fact that the central fifty minutes of the film are set entirely in and around the house, with only the central protagonists until the arrival of the two soldiers (rather than the interweaving narratives of most of his other output), this is many ways recognisable as a 'Téchiné film'. The war is here almost a pretext, or at most an extension of the workings of modernity in *J'embrasse pas*, juxtaposing, separating and recombining heterogeneous individuals. Like Lili in *Le Lieu du crime*, Odile is 'heterogenised', awakened to difference by the intruder from outside her world: at one point she describes herself as 'chavirée' (overwhelmed, 'capsized'), and as 'devenue quelqu'un que je ne connais pas' ('become someone I do not know') after the days, or weeks, spent in the house. The characters are marked, but not determined by, originary traumas: for the family, the loss of the husband and father in war, for Yvan his prison experiences and who knows what else, for all of them the killings on the road. (Yvan, despite of or because of his ease with nature and freedom, in fact is prone to fainting fits and panic attacks; on one occasion this occurs beneath telephone wires, connoting a connection to society and the real world, and therefore to confinement, a fact underlined by their parallel lines shot from his point of view as he lies in the grass.) The landscape, supposedly set further north but filmed in the southwest, is lovingly photographed by Agnès Godard. The idyll in the house constitutes another heterotopia in Téchiné's work, reached by a complex, initiatory procedure akin to the fairy stories told by Cathy. The four traverse a forest where they have to spend the night, they cross a stream, and Yvan plants a marker in a field to indicate the route to this enchanted castle – at a later point magically enveloped in mist – he had earlier successfully scouted. In the house, time – along with, as we shall see, history – is suspended. Yvan has cut the telephone wire and hidden the radio. Philippe has given Yvan his father's watch to persuade him to stay with them, and, guessing the time, resets a grandfather clock, incorrectly as it turns out. A memorable close-up of Odile in a moment of self-absorption in the bath, her face reflected in the water into which she sinks, recalls the link between heterotopia and the mirror we saw in *Les Roseaux sauvages*.

What is established in the house is a community or a family group without a father, in which sexuality is pluralised and redistributed, along with other social roles. Philippe, the middle-class would-be opera singer, is fascinated by Yvan the wild child, seeing him as a big brother he never had (a notion upsettingly ridiculed by Yvan), and with a hint of desire as it is he who undresses Yvan after one of his fits. The brother–sister relationship is an important reality for both boy and girl, although both Cathy and Philippe are also looking in other directions; she back to a world of animals and fantasy, and forward to marriage to her 'prince', Yvan, he forward to adult roles and the older boy. Yvan is both protector and vulnerable, adult and child. His costume is a bricolage of stolen clothes, a basque beret, an ill-fitting jacket, bright red underwear which, as the children comment, is more appropriate for a girl. Gaspard Ulliel's performance emphasises a body at ease in nature and in pleasure – the memorable bathing scene – but not at ease with itself, witness his awkward gait as he runs. Odile is the central figure, the mother struggling to protect her children, and to maintain order in a collapsing national, social and personal world. In this she is partly successful, imposing the rule on Yvan that if he wishes to stay she must keep his gun hidden. However, early in the film she had given into fear and wet herself like a child, and she uses childish language to Cathy in order to explain the stain: 'je me suis fait pipi dessus'. And by the time the outside world returns, she has been sufficiently 'dérangée' to reject the role and model of masculinity provided by one of the soldiers, a reassuring figure who is himself a father. Instead she runs to Yvan, whose sexual advances she had previously rejected. There follows the most explicit sex scene in any Téchiné film, and which provides one of the keys to Yvan's past. He holds a lighter up to Odile's naked body, for, he explains, he has never seen a woman's genitals. He then proceeds to have anal sex with her – 'c'est ce que je connais' ('this is what I know') – to which she assents. It is later revealed that Yvan's real name is Jean Delmas, and that in the chaos of the war he had escaped from the (in)famous penal colony at Mettray near Tours, established in 1839 and in fact closed before the war (in 1939) after a public campaign. The assumption is that until then he had experienced only same-sex activities, especially as Mettray is renowned in literary history as the place Jean Genet was confined for three years in the 1920s between the ages of 14 and 17. Rather than representing a teleological fulfilment in heterosexuality, the coupling between Odile and Yvan is in fact rather 'queered', in the sense that homosexual and heterosexual positions, gestures and histories come together, as it were, and 'heterogenise' each other.

The anal sex between Odile and Yvan is present in Gilles Perrault's novella. The fictional and journalistic output of Perrault (b. 1931) includes a film script for Michel Deville about a homosexual blackmail plot in the secret services, *Le Dossier 51* (1978). However, some significant differences between novella and film point to the distinctive take on the story by Taurand and Téchiné. The narration of *Les Egarés* is pluralised, so that although certain key shots are from Odile's point of view (of the first plane approaching in the attack scene, a loving gaze on the other three playing in the garden), there is no equivalent of the third-person narration centred on her consciousness in *Le Garçon aux yeux gris*. Indeed, it is Cathy's voiceover that narrates part of the film, including the opening words over the scene of refugees. The father is dead, unlike in the novella. In *Les Egarés*, much more is made of the relationships between the three other protagonists, their inner emotional lives (the little girl in Perrault cries most of the time), and of the isolation of the house, which becomes a kind of self-sufficient community at the border of nature and culture (in Perrault most of the food is obtained from raiding grocers' stores in villages).

Moreover, Taurand and Téchiné also choose to make alterations and additions which have wider, national implications. The absent owners of the house are Jewish musicians. Odile is a primary school-teacher (*institutrice*), and not an upper-middle-class housewife from the sixteenth *arrondissement*. Philippe agrees to sing for the French soldier, but the latter objects to his choice of a German *lieder*. And in Perrault, the soldiers are threatening brutes from whom Odile has to be rescued by Yvan, whereas in the film they are a well-behaved pair trying to make their way back to their native south. Another important difference introduces a (porous) duality which the film explores. For Perrault, the story was in part autobiographical, based on a memory of his experience in the *exode* when he was aged 9. For Téchiné, born in 1943, the events of June 1940 insert themselves into a memory after the fact, a 'postmemory' of sorts.

History and the national collectivity return like a vengeance in the film, signalled by a point of view shot through a car windscreen like those from Odile's point of view at the beginning. This time, however, it is the gaze of authority and administration, as the police car approaches the house. Yvan is handcuffed to a radiator, grid-like in its shape, facing a window, his back to the camera. At the refugee centre Odile is informed of his suicide in front of maps of France in a school classroom. In voiceover, Cathy narrates her disappointment that there will be no 14 July ceremonies this year (the Vichy regime was anti-republican), because she liked the fireworks. The central heterotopia of the film has therefore to be understood relationally, rather than as a lost idyll unfettered by political questions. Of course, these issues are partially sidestepped by the action of the film taking place during the *débâcle*, the fall of France and the very beginnings of the Vichy regime. Here the issue of Resistance versus collaboration, so urgently posed in turning-point film events such as Marcel Ophüls' *Le Chagrin et la pitié* (1969) and Louis Malle's *Lacombe Lucien* (1974), have not yet fully crystallised. However, *Les Egarés* joins that perennial problematic in French cinema since 1945: how to represent the war, into what national narrative to insert that representation, given that it was also a French civil war, and that until the 1970s Gaullism had determinedly constructed a myth of France as a nation of resisters? French cinema continues to return to these questions, as, periodically, does the French nation. The last paroxysm was the trial of Maurice Papon in 1997–78, the former Paris police chief and cabinet minister found guilty of sending 1,500 Jews to their deaths during the conflict. *Les Egarés* was contemporaneous with other films that revisited the war, such as Bertrand Tavernier's *Laissez-passer* (2002), about the wartime film industry, and Jean-Paul Rappeneau's *Bon Voyage* (2003), a farcical evocation of the government and French establishment's flight to Bordeaux in June 1940.

Within this corpus, an obvious intertext for *Les Egarés* is a film set during the exodus which opens with planes strafing refugees and which centres on children. *Jeux interdits* (René Clément, 1952) was made during a period located between that of the Liberation, which celebrated national collective action against the enemy, as in Clément's *La Bataille du rail* of 1945, and the 're-enchantment' of the

Resistance which came back with the return to power of De Gaulle in 1958 (Lindeperg 1997). In contrast, in *Jeux interdits* the *débâcle* is represented frankly, as are the pettiness and selfishness of ordinary French people caught up in the chaos. The film is thus about the disarray of ordinary individuals faced with the barbarism of war, which is denounced in general fashion via the contrast with the 'purity' of childhood. One contemporary French critic thus invoked Korea and Hiroshima in his discussion, rather than anything closer to home (Lindeperg 1997: 277).

Jeux interdits opens *in medias res*, with the column of refugees about to be attacked. The mode of filmmaking (in fact the sequence was filmed by the cinematographer Robert Juillard, who had experience of Italian neo-realism, working with Roberto Rossellini on *Germany Year Zero* of 1948) is characterised by numerous editing cuts, as shots of the refugees from various distances and angles are spliced together in staccato-like fashion to reproduce a sense of menace and the action of the guns. The emphasis is on collective apprehension of the events. The first close-up is of an anonymous woman screaming as she looks upward, and a reverse shot shows a bomb falling upon her which then explodes. Only gradually, in the relative calm following the first attack, does the camera home in on the family of little Paulette (Brigitte Fossey), photographing them from a couple of angles before the crowd loses patience with the stalled car and pushes it off the road and there is a first close-up of Paulette and her dog. This pattern is then repeated with the second attack, when a shot of an old lady, cowering at left of frame beside a tree with the carnage going on in the middle distance at right, alternates with the scene on the road, and the camera homes in again on the family as Paulette rushes on to the bridge to get her dog.

Téchiné's procedure quotes *Jeux interdits* in part, most notably when both families are seen cowering at the bottom of the frame while bullets or bombs hitting the ground approach them from top of frame. However, in these sequences in *Les Egarés* editing is also used much more to delineate individuals. The journey of Odile and her family had already been followed before the attacks via a variety of shots, including close-ups and through the car windscreen (the first is of her applying eye drops), and also via a much more mobile camera, establishing relations between the car's occupants, with the car itself and also with the world outside. Odile believes the car is a protective space, distinct from the chaos around them, upon which they can be spectators: hence the eye drops, and the early shot of Philippe looking out of the window on left of frame, as the refugee column proceeds cinematically outside on right of frame. Odile later refuses to let a wounded soldier enter. (This attempt at perpetuating bourgeois status in a moving vehicle will literally go up in flames, and finally the fixity of a bourgeois house will, paradoxically, produce mobility and openness despite her attempts to impose a similar order upon it.) Crane shots establish spatial relations within the column of refugees, partly in order to establish the context of the spectacle that is to come, and partly again to designate individuals who will then be seen to die, or, in the case of Yvan, emerge into the narrative. In *Jeux interdits*, the camera had moved only to follow vehicles (a plane diving, the car going into the ditch) or individuals already in movement (Paulette running across the bridge or walking along the riverbank, the dog being thrown into the water). While Téchiné also resorts to rapid editing in order to express the drama of the attack, it is from the point of view of Odile herself that the first plane is perceived.

Téchiné's procedure is much more novelistic in that he here seems to take the individual as starting-point, whereas in *Jeux interdits* the collectivity is the starting-point and in a sense remains so: Paulette's parents are dead, and although she ends up in a peasant community and forms a relationship with the slighter older Michel (Georges Poujouly), her status is really that of an icon of an abstract 'childhood', with resonances therefore of a wider 'humanity'. (In fact, this reproduces the standard chasm between childhood and adulthood which *Les Egarés* avoids.) Michael Kelly (2004) has argued that the category of the 'human' and the reinvocation of 'humanism' were instrumental in the ideological reconstruction of France during the Liberation period and into the early part of the Fourth Republic. (This contributed to the nation's blind spots over its colonial possessions.)

If Téchiné starts with individuals, he does not end with them. As we have seen, his films tend to articulate relations between protagonists that are seen both as socially/historically situated, and as particles or potentialities. Some may wish to argue for the allegorical 'national' character of the 'house' portrayed in *Les Egarés*, or at least of some of the stakes involved: the momentary federation of disparate social and geographical positions (including city–country, north–south, *institutrice* – primary schoolteachers were the shock troops of the regime during the early years of the Third Republic – and delinquent), the German song that both reiterates a boundary and aspires to a new or rediscovered internationalism. But given the efforts the film makes to mark out the house as a heterotopia, it seems more fruitful to seek the national question elsewhere, in the explorations *Les Egarés* makes of questions of memory and truth/falsehood.

The individuated narrative that is launched on the refugee road and in the family car does not constitute the first set of images of the film. Interspersed with the opening credits (white on black background, Philippe Sarde's theme playing first of all on that connotatively 'national' instrument, the accordion) are three silent archival images, of a bombed building collapsing, cavalry in disarray in a burning street, troops moving through a devastated city. Such images occur three more times. When Yvan hides the radio and listens in the cellar to the litany of names of lost children, a close-up of his face is followed by archive footage of a road filled with empty vehicles, apparently in the aftermath of a bombardment, and then of what seems to be his own memory of coming across a dead soldier whose possessions he takes. When one of the soldiers recalls to Odile the military defeat he witnessed, there is a cut from a close-up of his pensive face to black and white footage of a line of demoralised French troops. And when they all leave the house in the police car, archive footage of civilian life in the war serves as transition to their new life in the refugee centre. In the DVD interview, Téchiné emphasises the 'authenticity' of these archive images, in contrast to the distinctive space seemingly outside history constituted by the community in the house (Téchiné 2003). *Hôtel des Amériques* had similarly opened with archive footage of the town, emphasising interconnectedness and a collective history. However, in these post-traditional times, memory has of course a history. Whose memories are these? As Naomi Greene points out, drawing on Pierre Nora's work on *lieux de mémoire* or 'realms of memory':

> not only is modern memory lived as a 'duty' [or 'obligation'] and embodied in the 'archive' but – paradoxically – it is 'distanced' from the very past it strains to embrace [and has thus become] archival (*mémoire-archive*), obligatory (*mémoire-devoir*), and distanced (*mémoire-distance*). (Greene 1996: 118)

If memory has a history, then there are political stakes in its formulation, construction and perpetuation. In a famous interview with

Cahiers du cinéma in 1974, Michel Foucault found fault with recent films on the Second World War, for the way in which they evacuated the idea of popular struggle, and even the idea of Resistance which was hegemonic during the Gaullist era (Foucault 1974/1989).

In the context of 2003, we witness first of all in Téchiné's representation of the Second World War (but not in his earlier evocation of the Algerian war, as we have seen), an example of what Marianne Hirsch calls 'postmemory', which

> is distinguished from memory by generational distance and from history by deep personal connection. Postmemory is a powerful and very particular form of memory precisely because its connection to its object or source is mediated not through recollection but through an imaginative investment and creation ... Postmemory characterizes the experiences of those who grew up dominated by narratives that preceded their birth, whose own belated stories are evacuated by the stories of the previous generation shaped by traumatic events that can be neither understood nor recreated. (Hirsch 1997: 22)

Partly perhaps because his birth date bestrides this chronology, Téchiné in *Les Egarés* presents a hybrid view of the past, as *mémoire-archive*, postmemory, and as something else. The heterotopia in the film is momentarily suspended outside chronological time and history. In many ways the house becomes the fantasmatic projection of its inhabitants: the reconstitution of a domestic space for Odile, a realm of freedom for Yvan, an alternative family for Philippe, a magic kingdom for Cathy, a 'becoming-other' for everyone. This 'imaginative investment and creation' constitutes a virtual shadow accompanying the workings of society, history and politics, and is closely linked to the theme of lying and fabulation in the film.

Because the archive footage accompanies as well as opens and closes a heterotopic time and space that is moreover a realm of fantasies and stories, and therefore of different possible worlds, the notion of time in the film cannot be limited to questions of the historical 'truth' of 1940. This is what makes it so different from a film such as Jacques Audiard's *La Vie d'un héros* of 1996, in which the main character lies and passes himself off as a former resister in postwar France. If, as Gilles Deleuze argues, we are all within a world-memory rather than being limited by and to our own discrete 'memory' and therefore identity, then the Nietzschean idea of the 'power of the false' puts such truths in crisis: 'une puissance du faux qui remplace et détrône la forme du vrai, parce qu'elle pose la simultanéité de présents incompossibles, ou la coexistence de passés non-nécessairement vrais' (Deleuze 1985: 171) ('It is a power of the false which replaces and supersedes the form of the true, because it poses the simultaneity of incompossible presents, or the coexistence of not-necessarily true pasts'; Deleuze 1988: 131).

Yvan is a liar and a trickster. His ultimate goal is to be invisible or indiscernible, like a ghost (in some scenes he is filmed in a flowing white diaphanous shirt), or to blend with nature. But this is also the ambition of Cathy (he builds her a house made of branches, she talks to animals). In the final scene Philippe's hair is shaved like Yvan's (ostensibly against lice). And the upstanding Odile lies to the police, telling him that Yvan has escaped. This is a major change from the novella, in which Odile plants a knife in the police van so that Yvan can do just that. In the film, Yvan's death, and the accompanying lie, are part of a more mysterious ending that is nonetheless open and radical. The lie takes place, appropriately for this former *institutrice*, in a classroom. It is converted into a makeshift clinic but there are maps of France and also a blackboard, completely blank, that echoes the opening credits (in which 'Les Egarés' appears as if handwritten in white on a black background). Odile sits down in front of it as she reels emotionally from the news. There is a cut to Philippe, and the camera tracks him across the courtyard as he enters the classroom: she tells her version of Yvan's fate as Philippe is framed standing against the blackboard on the left, and she is sitting down on the right of frame with her back to a desk, with the maps of France in the background. This is all a reversal of the normal teacher–pupil, mother–son hierarchy. As she tells the lie, she stands up and begins to walk out of the room, accompanied by Philippe. She sits down on the ground next to Cathy in exactly the same position, and a crane shot films the courtyard and its activities through a wire fence, lingering on a man, whose only appearance in the film this is, as he stoops over, mixing cement with a trowel as construction work goes on around him. Rather than a simple image of 'reconstruction' – this is still very early in the war after all – the shot's suggestion of another story or of other stories to come that may or may not include Odile and her family is a clue to what kind of national idea or memory is being articulated in *Les Egarés*. In 2003, as opposed to 1945, 1952 or 1974, the most interesting notion of France and Frenchness, perhaps even more than that of an ongoing construction, is as something yet to be invented rather than as fully present. The 'impossible' house of *Les Egarés* is a France in minor mode, a term which Deleuze uses in relation to Third World cinemas (in which the people are 'lacking'), but which, quoting Jean-Louis Comolli, is also relevant for western societies: the impossibility of forming a group (a national community) and the impossibility of not doing so, 'l'impossibilité d'échapper au groupe et l'impossibilité de s'en satisfaire' (Deleuze 1985: 286) ('the impossibility of escaping from the group and the impossibility of being satisfied with it'; Deleuze 1988: 219). A key connotation of the star persona of Emmanuelle Béart has been linked to immigrant issues since March 1996, when she supported a hunger strike in a Paris church by illegal African immigrants – 'l'affaire des sans-papiers' – and images of her handcuffed to the protestors, and holding a black baby, were widely disseminated in the media. This is another reason why *Les Egarés* is to be compared not to the extensive corpus of French films set in the Second World War, but to works like *Les Innocents* and *Loin* which posit the nation as unfinished, and hint at a France yet to come.

References

Anderson, B. (1983). *Imagined Communities: Reflections on the Origin and Spread of Nationalism*. London, Verso.

Bhatia, N. (1996). Whither the Colonial Question: Jean Renoir's *The River*, in D.Sherzer (ed.), *Cinema, Colonialism, Postcolonialism: Perspectives from the French and Francophone World*. Austin, University of Texas Press, 51–64.

Bouquet, S. (1998). Martin n'est plus ici. *Cahiers du cinéma*, 529 (November), 73–74.

Butler, J. (1990). *Gender Trouble: Feminism and the Subversion of Identity*. London, Routledge.

Butler, J. (2000). *Antigone's Claim*. New York, Columbia University Press.

Deleuze, G. (1985). *Cinéma 2: L'Image-Temps*. Paris, Minuit.

Deleuze, G. (1988) *Cinema 2: The Time-Image*, translated by H. Tomlinson and R. Galeta. London, Athlone Press.

Deleuze, G. and F. Guattari (1980). *Mille plateaux: capitalisme et schizophrénie 2*. Paris, Minuit.

Deleuze, G. and F. Guattari (1988). *A Thousand Plateaus: Capitalism and Schizophrenia*, translated by B. Massumi. London, Athlone Press.

Foucault, M. (1974). Anti-rétro: Entretien avec Michel Foucault. *Cahiers du cinéma*, 251–252 (July–August), 5–15.

Foucault, M. (1989). Film and Popular Memory, translated by M.Jordin, in

Foucault Live (Interviews 1961–1984). New York, Semiotexte.

Frodon, J.-M. (1994). *Les Roseaux sauvages* d'André Téchiné. *Le Monde*, 1 June, 1.

Frodon, J.-M. (2000). Breakfasts with André Téchiné. *Le Monde*, 9–10 April, 12–13.

Greene, N. (1996). Empire as Myth and Memory, in D. Sherzer (ed.), *Cinema, Colonialism, Postcolonialism: Perspectives from the French and Francophone World*. Austin, University of Texas Press, 103–119.

Guichard, L. (2001). Les couleurs de Tanger. *Télérama*, 2662 (17 January), 24–26.

Hirsch, M. (1997). *Family Frames: Photography, Narrative and Postmemory*. Cambridge, MA, Harvard University Press.

Jones, K. (1997). *André Téchiné: la estrategía de la tensión*. Valladolid, Semana internacional de cine.

Jousse, T. and F. Strauss. (1994). Entretien avec André Téchiné. *Cahiers du cinéma*, 481 (June), 12–17.

Kelly, M. (2004). *The Cultural Reconstruction of France in the Aftermath of World War II*. London, Palgrave.

Kaganski, S. (2001). André Téchiné – Tangente à Tanger. *Les Inrockuptibles* (28 August). www.lesinrocks.com/DetailArticle.cfm?iditem=129754.

Lindeperg, S. (1997). *Les Ecrans de l'ombre: la seconde guerre mondiale dans le cinéma français (1944–1969)*. Paris, CNRS Editions.

Mendras, H. (1988). *La Seconde Révolution française*. Paris, Gallimard

Mendras, H. (1991). *Social Change in Modern France*, with A. Cole. Cambridge University Press.

Perrault, G. (2001). *Le Garçon aux yeux gris*. Paris, Fayard.

Philippon, A (1988). *André Téchiné*. Paris, Cahiers du cinéma.

Rochu, G. and Y.Salhi (1996). De la corruption au populisme: Toulon ville amiral du Front national. *Le Monde diplomatique* (July), 4–5.

Ross, K. (1995). *Fast Cars, Clean Bodies: Decolonization and the Reordering of French Culture*. Cambridge, MA, MIT Press.

Sophocles (1984). *The Three Theban Plays*, translated by R. Fagles. London, Penguin.

Téchiné, A. (1996). Le Dépaysement humain (Interview). *Nouvelle Revue Française*, 520 (May), 41–57.

Téchiné, A. (2003). *Les Egarés*. Interview. Paris, Wildside Video.

White, A. (1995). Strange Gifts: André Téchiné Remakes the Melodrama. *Film Comment*, 31 (July), 70–75.

Žižek, S. (1991). *For They Know Not What They Do: Enjoyment as a Political Factor*. London, Verso.

5

Collaborations

Les Temps qui changent (2004)

Téchiné's sixteenth and latest film, centred as it is on its two stars, is a useful point of departure for examining the collaborative nature of his work, and shows the extent to which an approach excessively centred on the director as *auteur* risks missing wider creative processes. The subject matter of *Les Temps qui changent* is echoed in its procedure. Antoine, a French engineer (Gérard Depardieu), travels to Tangiers to supervise the construction of buildings for a new television station in the 'free zone'. His real motivation, however, is to seek out his first love from thirty years before, Cécile (Catherine Deneuve), who works at a radio station and is married to a Moroccan Jewish doctor, Natan (Gilbert Melki). Cécile and Natan's son Sami (Malik Zidi) visits from Paris with his neurotic and drug-dependent girlfriend Nadia (Lubna Azabal) and her young son Saïd (Jabir Elomri). Sami spends much of his time with his lover Bilal (Nadem Rachati), who is looking after a villa for its absent owners. Nadia is desperate to see her identical twin sister Aïcha (also played by Azabal), who is reluctant to see her, lives alone in Tangiers, is religious and conservative, wears a headscarf, and works in McDonalds, where Nadia gets her only glimpse of her. Natan has been having extra-marital affairs, Cécile's marriage has been increasingly loveless, and she eventually succumbs to Antoine's advances, initially proposing a 'brief stop' ('une halte') on life's road rather than his preference for them to end their days together, and they make love. But Antoine is left in a coma after a landslide on the building site. Cécile and Natan separate (it is suggested he takes up with Aïcha), Bilal refuses to take up Sami's offer of a trip to Paris, to which Sami, Nadia and Saïd return. Months later, after she has visited him in hospital seemingly every day, Cécile sees Antoine wake up, and their hands join.

The film explores the relationship between past and present, not only in the central quest and love story, but also in its recapitulation of motifs and scenes from previous Téchiné films: it asks of both these strands, in the context of encroaching old age and, beyond that, of death itself, what are the possibilities for renewal, what relationship is possible between those past 'sediments' and the open future. In this way, the film restages Téchiné's simultaneous attentiveness to socio-historical determinants and strata, and also to desires, dreams, aspirations, a virtual realm completely distinct from the antiseptic computer-generated animated film that advertises the new media complex. For this reason Antoine's accident acquires a kind of mythical status: the scene is repeated three times, opening the film before the flashback to his arrival, filmed in 'real time' within the main narrative chronology, and just preceding his reawakening in hospital, when it is part of Antoine's mental world. The symbolic burial, preceded by Antoine inspecting the state of the ground and its layers, takes place on a construction site, combining ideas of old and new, death and renewal, even rebirth. The substance of the mudslide is not altogether solid, as both Antoine's point of view and that of the neutral camera position emphasise particles, bits of earth as they fall into a pool of water like raindrops.

While the 'event' of the film is the reunion of the two *monstres sacrés* of French cinema – to whom we shall return – and that central love story dominated by existential awareness of time, the stars are located in a network of stories and relationships, in a plural fashion typical of Téchiné. We thus return to the Tangiers of *Loin*, the frontier city, with two of the actresses from that film: Lubna Azabal, and Nabila Baraka, who plays Antoine's assistant Nabila. Scenes filmed in its crowded and noisy streets, and the liminal space of the airport, alternate with interior scenes at the workplace, in Antoine's hotel room and Cécile and Natan's home. The city is filmed as in constant transformation: a mechanical digger is working even in sight of the family house. Combining the versatility and lightness of the digital camera used in *Loin* with the visual advantages of 35mm, a hand- or shoulder-held camera was used to accentuate the film's sense of mobility, its opening out of the protagonists' inner, mental and emotional lives.

For Téchiné, this amounted to filming a psychological 'art' movie like an action film: 'J'ai choisi de filmer cette histoire comme un film d'action, pas comme un petit théâtre intime, en ce sens que dans un film d'action les personnages sont en mouvement et les sentiments en action. Il fallait rendre visible tout ce qui unit et tout ce qui sépare les personnages'.[1] This is particularly striking in the seemingly closed set of Cécile's living room: she is working with Rachel at the computer when Antoine calls unexpectedly, and the mobile camera captures the shifting possibilities of relations within this restricted space, as the three are then joined by Natan coming out of the swimming pool. The scene then settles down to film the four in frame and to play on the relationship, in terms of glances and soundtrack, between foreground (Antoine and Natan drinking whisky and discussing his medical case) and background (Cécile and her friend and colleague Rachel – played by Tanya Lopert, the mother from *Les Innocents* – discussing work).

Other material is also familiar. A scene at the casino, as in *Hôtel des Amériques*, emphasises the twin motifs of money and chance. Cultural identities are complex, as Natan points out about his own. Bilal maps out Sami's reality by describing him as 'half-French, half-Moroccan, half-man, half-woman'. The same-sex relationship is portrayed in a relaxed manner (the first hint of same-sex desire is a lingering shot from Sami's point of view on a group of young men in a car), the issue between him and Bilal being one of economic inequality. Sami, Nadia and Saïd constitute an alternative family structure. The 'doubling' embodied by the identical twins Nadia and Aïcha is a graphic rendering of how in Téchiné different possible destinies hover and coexist. Antoine's status as 'revenant' – someone who has come back, one of the words in French for 'ghost' – means that he confronts Cécile with precisely that alternative. Juliette Garrigues signs the musical score, as in *Loin*, and Angélique Kidjo is here used three times in the diegesis: the haunting 'Okan Bale' plays over the credits but is also the song played at Cécile's radio station after she has thrown Antoine out, the camera lingering on her ambiguous

1 'I wanted to film the story like an action film, not like a piece of intimate theatre, meaning that in an action film the characters are in movement and feelings in action. Everything that brings together or separates the characters had to be made visible'; Mérigeau 2004. See also the interview with his chief cinematographer Julien Hirsch, who had been assistant cinematographer on *Loin* and who had worked with Jean-Luc Godard on *Eloge de l'amour* and *Notre Musique*: Frodon 2004.

expression; the dance track 'Tumba' accompanies the family party at the swimming pool; and as Antoine prepares for bed in his hotel room he listens to Cécile's programme play Kidjo's version of Serge Gainsbourg's 'Ces Petits Riens', a melancholic play on the word 'rien' ('anything', 'nothing') in the context of unrequited love.[2]

As in *Ma Saison préférée*, the film is very self-conscious about ageing but also the different stages of an individual's life and the play of persistence and disappearance of past selves. This is nowhere more apparent than in the film's treatment of childhood: Saïd is by far the most cheerful of all the characters, apart possibly from Rachel, but the child lives on in the adults. Twice Saïd's body is filmed as an extension of an adult's, as he clings to Natan's back as he teaches him to swim, and as Sami – always affectionate in the scenes with him – carries him on his shoulders through a crowd. The first event when Sami returns to his family home is for his childhood toys to fall out of the cupboard in his old bedroom. And the behaviour of Antoine, the besuited westerner who has 'succeeded in life', is childlike.

This is most clearly illustrated in the scene of his first encounter with Cécile in the film. At the start of a two-minute sequence, the shoulder-held camera pans round a jeweller's display, vertically to a shot of the shop assistant and Antoine as he tries to select a gift for her, and then down once more to a still photograph of Cécile when she was younger. A brief shot-reverse shot films the uncomprehending face of the Moroccan jeweller, suggesting gaps, between cultures, but also between Antoine's desires and 'reality'. The camera then follows him through the shopping centre, filming him from in front as he walks past a row of supermarket checkouts. A point of view shot and edit capture his first glimpse of Cécile – in this prosaic setting, and with her husband – and the camera then rapidly pans back to him as he runs towards the right, following him as he hides behind a potted plant, two point of view shots repeated through the foliage. Antoine moves to his right to sit down, and another edit shows his point of view, of a little boy sucking a lollipop on his mother's lap. After another point of view shot of Cécile and her husband, he decides to leave, and the camera follows him from behind, an edit to him looking is this time not followed by a point of view shot, he continues walking and the camera shoots him walking into a glass door, as he

2 'Mieux vaut ne penser à rien Que de penser à vous' ('Better to think of nothing than to think of you').

mistakes his own projection for 'reality'. His loss of any control is emphasised by the point of view shots – of the crowd and Natan, who rushes to his aid – being now turned on him. Looked after by Natan, who is filmed to his left, slightly above him, he announces that he is going to 'shit himself' ('j'ai la chiasse'). It is at that moment that he sees Cécile walking towards him, aghast: her walk towards him is marked by three fades, syncopations of time, but the extreme close-up of his face is followed by a cut to his hands, as he struggles to locate his glasses. The gesture summarises the coexistence of the child, the desiring young man, and the ageing body.

At one point, partly on Natan's insistence, Cécile drives Antoine outside the city in order to view a property to rent. The first part of the sequence reproduces in simpler fashion the use of the car as capsule of time to be found in *Ma Saison préférée*. Cécile is driving: shots alternate between them, first from Antoine to her, and then of both of them with him on left of frame and she on the right. The foliage of the countryside moving backwards is captured behind their figures through the car windows, but is also projected on to their bodies via the reflection in the glass. The car breaks down, and the shoulder-held camera follows them out of the vehicle. Cécile, despite her knowledge of car mechanics, is unable to fix it. Antoine declares helplessly, 'Alors, qu'est-ce qu'on fait?' ('So, what do we do now?'). They decide to press on on foot to view the house, and are filmed through foliage walking through the woods. The emphasis at this stage in the film is on the disparity between them, in terms of their views of the world and of their relationship. In their dialogue, continuing the image of the car in motion, time is rendered in spatial terms: for Cécile, 'la passion est derrière nous' ('passion is behind us'). There is disagreement on what is 'devant nous' ('in front of us'): for Cécile it is a void, the cliff and the sea, for Antoine however the scene is a plenitude of ever-increasing circles: the sea, a ferry, mist, Spain, Europe.

For Antoine, the woods are also a potential source of enchantment: he says he would like them to get lost together within them. His hope represents the possibility of creating there the same kind of hetero-topias that were – briefly – created in the countryside of *Les Roseaux sauvages* and *Les Egarés*, coupled with an embedded childlike sense of the fairytale and of wonderment. Antoine had gone to Nabila to seek her advice on local sorcery and spells to make Cécile love him again; to this end he had placed a photograph of their younger selves under

her bed. This theme of the disjunctions to be found in the historical embedding of the society depicted (here, a rapidly transforming
Morocco, but it can apply to western societies too) is what underpins
the trope, in Latin American culture and elsewhere, of 'magic realism',
which for Fredric Jameson results from 'the overlap or the coexistence of precapitalist and nascent capitalist or technological features'.
Films and other texts articulate a 'superposition of whole layers of
the past within the present' (Jameson 1992: 138–139). We have seen
that in most of Téchiné, the social and historical 'real', and with it an
emotional and melodramatic narrative, is not abandoned in favour
of intensities in the present. Rather, the real and virtual inform and
accompany each other. This is vividly illustrated in the scene which
closes the sequence of Antoine and Cécile in the woods.

On the cliff edge, with the sea behind them, the pair come across
a large group of black Africans, would-be clandestines seeking to
cross to Europe. The pair walk from right to left of frame, and then,
after they have left the frame altogether, the camera lingers for a few
seconds on the group, with a baby visible, its cries audible on the
soundtrack. The practical Cécile comments on the precariousness
of their situation, vulnerable as they are to police raids – she later
witnesses with Rachel a clandestine being arrested – and robberies.
While she is understood in the film – and named by Natan – as a
'feminist', and understands, unlike Antoine, the political stakes in his
media centre project (a pro-western Arab TV station that will counter
Al-Jazeira), her relationship with Moroccan culture(s) is in many ways
limited: she does not speak Arabic, and the constant references in
newsroom or media chatter in the film to the situation in Iraq can be
understood as 'background', or ironic counterpoint to the love story,
or a comment on the ways in which they are both lost or adrift in their
lives and events: in any case neither she nor Antoine interacts with it.
In contrast, Antoine draws general conclusions from the presence of
the clandestines. For the first time in the sequence, he takes charge
of the situation and walks ahead of Cécile, reassuring her that the
clandestines represent no danger to them. He rather narcissistically
projects on to them an aspect of his own agenda: the reason for their
survival is that they have a 'goal', that of course of reaching Europe.
Then he adds; 'ici c'est la dernière étape avant le paradis' ('this is the
final stop before paradise').

In *Loin*, the clandestines were filmed in the urban chaos of

Tangiers, in Sara's hotel, or at the entry to the docks. Their presence in the luminous setting of the woods overlooking the sea is an effective re-entry of social and historical processes into the text and texture of *Les Temps qui changent*, but it also partakes of the film's virtual and mythical dimensions. Although Antoine had been indifferent to Nabila's proposals for some tourism in the area, including a visit to Hercules' cave, his invocation here of 'paradise' hints not only at his own ageing and death but also at the mythical dimensions of the film's play on aspirations, dreams, time and historical embedding that are afforded by the setting. For the south side of the straits of Gibraltar was associated with one of the classical versions of 'paradise', namely the Garden of the Hesperides from which Hercules had to retrieve the golden apple as one of his twelve labours. The other classical reference in the film is when Cécile reads to Saïd from *The Odyssey*, in fact from Book X. This opens with the visit to the floating island of Aeolia, where King Aeolus presides over his twelve sons and daughters whom he has joined in marriage. More than this quaintly alternative family structure – with its total endogamy – the reference is significant for Aeolus' mastery of the winds: he gives Ulysses a wineskin containing all the winds but one, that which will take him back to Ithaca. Ulysses' sailors, however, release the other winds too soon and they are once again sent off-course. *The Odyssey* adds a mythical, and possibly bathetic, dimension to Antoine's own goal-oriented love narrative (he implies in the scene in the woods that he has been searching for Cécile for years, and explains how difficult it was to get a post in Tangiers); but the reference to Aeolia is also significant for this film's spatial rendition of time, and its plural plotting. Aeolia is the place where the winds – and therefore the different directions of maritime space – converge and then are launched again to form new voyages, and narratives. Book X of *The Odyssey* also recounts Ulysses' arrival on Telepylus, land of the giant and cannibalistic Laestrygonians who destroy most of Ulysses' fleet and massacre most of his men. This is the story which Saïd remembers the next day when he asks Sami about giants, only to be told that there are no giants now, only 'dwarves', so that all people are now basically the same height. This 'disenchantment' of the world is immediately followed by a 're-enchantment': Saïd, sitting on Sami's shoulders, is enabled to 'fly', as the young man stretches his arms apart and runs up steps, to giggles from the boy.

Stars

Despite the film's typical pluralism, it is the reunion of Deneuve and Depardieu which is at the centre of the film, along with the central love story and love quest. The two stars first appeared together in François Truffaut's *Le Dernier Métro* (1980), then in Alain Corneau's *Le Choix des armes* (1981) and *Fort Saganne* (1984), and François Dupeyron's *Drôle d'endroit pour une rencontre* (1988). Depardieu's half-comic, childlike and at the same time understated performance is consistent in *Les Temps qui changent* with a self-consciousness about time, identity and modernity. Those who find far-fetched the quest for a love lost thirty years ago might reflect on the contemporary phenomenon of websites such as Friends Reunited, which seem to respond to widely felt needs for connection, be it through electronic and digital media. This is analogous to the record-request show on which Cécile works, which puts friends and families in touch via the radio, and to which Antoine of course listens in his hotel room; Antoine also uses a voice recorder to rehearse his messages to Cécile, and it of course possesses the capacity to reverse or accelerate time. But such nostalgia – and what is nostalgia if not the hovering of a virtual world alongside the real, with the relation between the two capable of being static or dynamic – also speaks to a desire to 'step out' of adult responsibility and stress (the contrast between Antoine's working life and his amorous plotting is staggering). In the film, still photographs are the index for the process of ageing, and for recapturing but also overcoming lost time. At the jewellers', Antoine uses a still black and white photo of the young Cécile to help choose correctly, to some incomprehension from the shop owner, as we have seen; and in an attempt to 'envoûter' ('cast a spell on') Cécile, he sneaks into her bedroom to place a photograph of their young selves under the mattress. It is only when Cécile discovers and burns it that he wakes up from his coma. These images foreground of course issues concerning the two actors and their star personae: *Les Temps qui changent* is also about stardom, the history of cinema, the history of audiences watching Deneuve and Depardieu, and even the itinerary of the director himself. Notably, the still photograph hidden then burned in the film is a well-known publicity still from the late 1970s, with François Truffaut – cropped out here of course – standing on their right.

Téchiné's films feature an extensive use of still photographs. As Nina/Juliette Binoche in *Rendez-vous* reads from *Romeo and Juliet*, she uses as a bookmark a photograph of the dead Quentin/Lambert Wilson (this is before his reappearance in the film as a 'ghost'); the film contrasts this photography with the instrumental polaroids associated with the estate agents'. In *Les Innocents*, photos pinpoint an identity that is then problematised (Saïd/Abdel Kechiche's first approach to Jeanne/Sandrine Bonnaire), represent a virtual world to be aspired to (Alain/Stéphane Onfroy's Algerian landscapes pinned to the wall), but also death and loss (the hotel owner's framed photo of her dead husband). This association with death is the dominant mode of Evelyne/Hélène Vincent's portrait of her younger self in Djakarta, alongside her dead father, which she shows to Pierre/Manuel Blanc in *J'embrasse pas*, and of that of Maïté/Elodie Bouchez's absent father in New Caledonia which she shows to Henri/Frédéric Gorny. In *Les Egarés*, the same connotations are complicated by the fact that the still photos are of a family that in 1940 is absent (from their house occupied by the refugees), but which, from the point of view of the 2003 audience, is dead, and very possibly, as their name is 'Weil', murdered in the Holocaust. *Ma Saison préférée*, as self-conscious about ageing as *Les Temps qui changent*, marks the apogee of this link between still photos and what has passed, as they are placed in the three homes of the family members, and their scrutiny is usually motivated in the narrative (looked at by a character in the diegesis): when Berthe/Marthe Villalonga collapses in the orchard, there is a cut from her face to a montage of still photographs of her past life (her memory is constituted by photographs, they are an extension of those on display in her house); Antoine/Daniel Auteuil, a character lost in time as we have seen, wakes up on the sofa at his mother's home, a shot preceded and followed by close-ups of stills of them and his sister Emilie/Deneuve in past time, accompanied by a conversation in which he underlines, in a very Proustian fashion, the temporal confusion caused by sleep, particularly in that setting, and the effort needed to remember his life and identity after he left home; later in the film he shows a photograph of their younger selves to his sister, but she has already fallen asleep and it is still on the bed when he returns to her the next day. In *Les Voleurs*, the obsessional, controlling Alex/Auteuil takes a photograph of Marie/Deneuve – who later commits suicide – when she is sleeping, and keeps a frame of it. In *Alice et Martin*, a family album circulates as part of the narrative of property and filiation: shown by his father to the young Martin, it is then looked at by the adult on the day of his brother's funeral, but then most of the photographs, of Martin as a child, are returned to his mother, signalling his eventual extrication from his paternal family's grip.

The association between still photographs and death to be found in Téchiné is very close to that outlined by his friend Roland Barthes in *La Chambre claire/Camera Lucida* (1980, the year of Barthes's own death). For Barthes, the dominant aspect of the still photograph is temporal: the capturing and reproduction of 'that which was' ('le ça-a-été'), and which will not be again, and even 'that which will be and has been', a future anterior. The experience of being photographed is that of a subject becoming an object, 'une micro-expérience de la mort' (Barthes 1980: 28) ('A micro-experience of death', Barthes 1984: 14). This 'magic' and 'spectral' aspect to photography, which in the past expressed itself in an obsession with doubles, is concealed, dealt with in fact, by the generalisation and banalisation of the photographic image in modernity (as with Martin's commodified image in *Alice et Martin*). Barthes is at times ambivalent about the relation between still photography and cinema, arguing that the two are very different, as in photos there is no 'offscreen' space, and that the spectral poses of past time are in cinema recuperated by the continuous movement of the images, but also noting that 'the melancholy of photography' reasserts itself when in a film he sees actors who are now dead (Barthes 1980: 124; Barthes 1984: 79).

Téchiné maintains these binaries but at the same time works with them. He deploys ghosts and doubles to signal other possible worlds. Most of the still images in his films connote dead past time, but the same can be said of his insertion of the 8mm home movie in *Le Lieu du crime* (scenes from an unhappy marriage, and of the son as infant, that are now left behind), the war footage in *Les Egarés*, and the newsreels of Biarritz in *Hôtel des Amériques*, whose charm is analogous to Barthes's fascination with Jacques Lartigue's 1931 series of photographs of the town ('maybe I was there'; Barthes 1980: 130; Barthes 1984: 83). Moreover, the extensive use in *Ma Saison préférée* and *Les Temps qui changent* of photos of performers when they were younger creates a dynamic relationship between still and moving image, and between the twin poses that cinema fleetingly captures of the 'actor' and that of his or her 'role'. As Barthes pointed out, the age of photography coincided with 'l'irruption du privé dans le public, ou plutôt à la création d'une nouvelle valeur sociale, qui est la publicité du privé; le privé est consommé comme tel, publiquement' (Barthes 1980: 153).[3] When Cécile burns the photograph at the end of *Les Temps qui changent*, she destroys Antoine's fixation on a lost youth and past that cannot be recaptured, but she is also giving him what he wants, that she be at his side; so the 'pose of the role' is subsumed, literally consumed, in fire, by the future-directed moving images. At the same time, the 'pose of the actor' is also being burned, in a way which signals the reality and inevitability of death (as fire accelerates time), but which moreover comments on and integrates the previous star images of the now 56-year-old Gérard Depardieu and 61-year-old Catherine Deneuve, delivering for them, at the same time as they publicly age, an open future typical of Téchiné.[4]

Catherine Deneuve has made more films (five) with André Téchiné than with any other director she has worked with in her long career. Jacques Demy, that other filmmaker of movement in social and mental worlds, is the only other director with whom she has made more than two films. Born in the same year (1943), Téchiné had for long hoped to work with Deneuve before they were brought together by their mutual agent Gérard Lebovici. Secondary texts and interviews frequently emphasise the 'complicity' between actress and director:

> André m'a beaucoup aidée à aller dans une direction que je pressentais en moi mais où, sans lui, je ne serais pas forcément allée aussi rapidement. Il m'a fait gagner du temps. Il m'a beaucoup poussée vers une certaine forme de nudité, de vérité, quelque chose qui, dans mon jeu, est à la fois plus simple et plus complexe.[5]

3 'the explosion of the private into the public, or rather the creation of a new social value, which is the publicity of the private; the private is consumed as such – publicly' (Barthes 1984: 98).

4 Depardieu's own comments on the place of *Les Temps qui changent* in his current work are interesting from this point of view: 'C'est un peu ma situation dans le cinéma: il y a des gros films qui me poussent, de grosses conneries, et j'essaye de renaître d'une autre façon, peut-être en travaillant avec Téchiné, en faisant le pas de côté' ('It's a bit like my place in cinema: my work is driven by big productions, that are in fact bollocks, and then I try to be reborn in a different way, maybe by working with Téchiné, and stepping into another way of doing things'): de Baecque and Lefort 2004.

5 'André helped me a lot to move in another direction that I thought I had in me but which I would not necessarily have taken without him. He saved me time. He encouraged me in a certain form of nakedness and truth, something at once simpler and more complex in my performance': from a 1998 interview with

Deneuve has even described Téchiné as a kind of 'brother'.[6] Indeed, that complicity seems to extend to Deneuve taking an active role in the creative process of Téchiné's films. Martine Giordano, Téchiné's regular editor, has recounted that Deneuve convinced him to retain the scene in *Le Lieu du crime* in which Thomas meets the killer of his mother/Deneuve's lover just after he has seen the couple having sex (Philippon 1988: 141). And Julien Hirsch, Téchiné's cinematographer on *Les Temps qui changent*, tells how Deneuve would view all the dailies, and was 'bien plus que l'interprète principale: une formidable partenaire de création pour André' ('much more than the main actress: a tremendous creative partner for André') (Frodon 2004: 21). It is also intriguing that the first of the five films she has made with Téchiné coincided with the 'realist turn' in his output, and a new relationship with actors.

The Téchiné–Deneuve collaboration amounts to that of director and *acteur-fétiche*, in the sense of a performer who has forged a particular relationship with a director and who repeatedly appears in their *œuvre*, or in a particular period of it. That relationship, and its associated meanings, may emerge from one or more of the following: shared aesthetic priorities, a shared cultural or generational habitus, projection or identification on to the performer, a 'fit' between performance style/appearance and film projects, personal or sexual involvement. Téchiné takes aspects of Deneuve's star persona (bourgeois glamour; the innocent–sexual, 'fire–ice' dichotomy; the federating of national discourses), and of her acting style, and reworks them for his purposes. She is relatively de-glamorised (*Le Lieu du crime, Ma Saison préférée*), and placed in narratives of transformation, exchange, and 'becoming-other', in which, in a residual Brechtian move, the audience is invited to explore the social contradictions which produce the gap between her iconicity and her role. She is placed in a (poly)sexual economy and (homosexual) regime of looking very different from, for example, the male heterosexual gaze offered by François Truffaut: in *La Sirène du Mississippi/Mississippi Mermaid* (1969), she is both a mysterious

---

Deneuve in *Studio magazine*, quoted in Fache 2004: 257. See also Deneuve/Téchiné, l'amour à deux 1993.

6 In *Télérama* (1997): 'Je n'ai pas eu de frère dans la vie non plus. Alors, je m'en suis choisi un: c'est André' ('I didn't have a brother in real life either. So I chose one: André'), http://toutsurdeneuve.free.fr/Francais/Pages/Carriere_Partenaires/ Techine.htm.

and deceiving *femme fatale* in relation to the male hero, and in the end the forgiven bearer of a transcendent love; in *Le Dernier Métro*, she is the recipient (as 'enigma' and object of desire) of a voyeuristic and, at the end, of a would-be transcendent fetishistic gaze which 'resolves' away contradiction. Her persona, particularly the cultural capital it embodies, throws into particular relief Téchiné's preference for placing together heterogenous social elements, and to have his characters shift between background and foreground. The melancholic (less often mentioned in star studies of her are the connotations of the tragic and public loss of her sister Françoise Dorléac in a car accident in 1967, which colour perceptions of her 'distance') and enigmatic aspects of her persona, and also the understatement of her performance, also nourish Téchiné's interest in the relationship between the virtual and the actual. In fact he has stated his preference in directing actors for 'ceux qui jouent sur ce qu'ils cachent' to 'ceux qui jouent sur ce qu'ils montrent'. This 'dénuement du jeu ... où l'on dégage un potentiel intérieur' is what he admires in Deneuve: 'Catherine serait plutôt sur la réserve, il semble qu'elle a toujours des choses à dévoiler, qu'elle n'a jamais atteint un plafond'.[7]

Actors, screenwriters, producers, editors

There is no doubt that Téchiné's collaboration with Deneuve is his most significant with an actor, although he has in the past returned to other stars, having made two films each with Isabelle Adjani, Daniel Auteuil, Emmanuelle Béart, Juliette Binoche, Jean-Claude Brialy and Gérard Depardieu. However, as well as those stars who in a sense 'transcend their profession' (Téchiné 1996), and the example of Marthe Villalonga, well established in popular comedy before the first of her three darker castings in *Les Innocents*, *Ma Saison préférée* and *Alice et Martin*, he tends to prefer those starting out on their career (Binoche in *Rendez-vous*, the team of young actors in *Les Roseaux sauvages*), and, often in minor roles, a trusted group who at times are a kind of repertory company for Téchiné: Roschdy Zem (*J'embrasse pas*, *Ma Saison*

---

7 'those who base their performance on what they hide' to 'those who base it on what they show'. This 'denuding of performance allows an inner potential to emerge'; 'Catherine is rather reserved, it seems there is always something to be revealed in her, that she has never reached her ceiling', Téchiné 1996: 42–43.

préférée, Alice et Martin), Eric Kreikenmayer (*Les Roseaux sauvages, Les Voleurs, Alice et Martin, Les Egarés*) and especially Michèle Moretti, whose collaboration with Téchiné goes as far back as Marc'O's theatre group in the 1960s (*Paulina s'en va, Souvenirs d'en France, Rendez-vous, J'embrasse pas, Ma Saison préférée, Les Roseaux sauvages*).

Téchiné always writes his own screenplays, but always in collaboration with at least one other. He has worked regularly with two former *Cahiers* critics who are now film directors: Pascal Bonitzer (*Les Sœurs Brontë, Le Lieu du crime, Les Innocents, Ma Saison préférée, Les Temps qui changent*), who has also done extensive work with Jacques Rivette, and whose directorial credits include the comedy *Rien sur Robert* (1999); and Olivier Assayas (*Rendez-vous, Le Lieu du crime, Alice et Martin*), whose films are a mixture of social observation (*Fin août, début septembre*/*Late August, Early September*, 1998; *Les Destinées sentimentales*, 2000), and an opening out on to other world (Asian) cinemas (*Irma Vep*, 1996; *Demonlover*, 2002). The third most important writing collaborator is Gilles Taurand (*Hôtel des Amériques, Les Roseaux sauvages, Les Voleurs, Alice et Martin, Les Egarés*), who worked with Raúl Ruiz on the screenplay of *Le Temps retrouvé*/*Time Regained* (1999), and with Robert Guédiguian on *Le Promeneur du Champ de Mars*/*The Last Mitterrand* (2005).[8]

The other crucial figure in this writing constellation is Jacques Nolot, whom Téchiné met through Roland Barthes. Born, like Téchiné, in 1943 in the south-west of France, he has appeared in small roles in six of Téchiné's films: *Hôtel des Amériques* (as one of the cruising homosexuals in the park), *Rendez-vous, Le Lieu du crime* (as the priest), *Les Innocents, Ma Saison préférée* and *Les Roseaux sauvages* (as the replacement teacher). Elsewhere, his most high-profile acting role in recent years has been in François Ozon's *Sous Le Sable*/*Under the Sand* (2000). More notably, he starred in the adaptation Téchiné

8 I indicate these to emphasise the collaborative dimension of Téchiné's output, and to flag up for future work the role of the scriptwriter, rather than, fruitlessly, to attempt to sort out the 'origin' of individual inputs. However, in an interview with Kent Jones (1997: 169–176), Assayas has stressed the interest he shares with Téchiné in both cinematic form and narrative, and how he learned from him how to write for actors. He also describes how *Rendez-vous* was truly written jointly, but how Téchiné was the 'architect' of *Le Lieu du crime*, with an idea for each scene, and how then the three collaborators took turns in writing a scene. Gilles Taurand and Téchiné write together at the same computer: Blumenfeld 1998.

made of his play *La Matiouette* for the small screen, and he was the co-scriptwriter on *J'embrasse pas*, in which the character of Romain/ Philippe Noiret is partly based on Barthes. Nolot's original version of the script much more explicitly placed Pierre in an underground and violent gay milieu, with the main character meeting an HIV-positive man who helped him to kill his pimp (De Baecque and Bouquet 1998: 26). His play *Le Café des Jules* was adapted for the screen by Paul Vecchiali in 1989.[9] Nolot's first feature film as director, *L'Arrière Pays* (1998), won much critical acclaim, and can be seen as the third part of a triptych along with his two projects with Téchiné. In it a gay middle-aged actor, played by Nolot himself (reversing the casting of *La Matiouette*), returns to his native village in the south-west (Nolot's own home village of Marciac, with locals playing many of the roles) on the illness and death of his mother. This simultaneously hyper-naturalistic and discreet work explores the rituals, conviviality and also (familial and collaborationist) secrets of the rural community.[10] Nolot's second feature, *La Chatte à deux têtes* (2002) is set in a porn cinema. Téchiné and Nolot collaborated again in 2001 when Nolot played the lead role as a Moroccan café owner in *Le Café de la plage*, which was co-scripted by Téchiné along with the film's director, Benoît Graffin. (Téchiné's other scriptwriting collaboration in this period was in 1997 on *Transatlantique*, directed by Christine Laurent – regular scriptwriter for Jacques Rivette along with Bonitzer – which starred Laurence Côte as a Frenchwoman looking for her lover in a decaying, post-dictatorship Montevideo.[11])

The other directorial spin-off from Téchiné's *œuvre* has been that of Gaël Morel, who appeared as François in *Les Roseaux sauvages* and *Loin*. His three theatrical features have acquired international distribution, and in a more visceral manner than Téchiné explore contemporary masculinities and marginal French identities, notably through reference to youth, homosexuality and the North African dimension. *A toute vitesse/Full Speed* (1996), on which Téchiné was technical adviser, casts (as in his 1999 TV film *Premières neiges*) Elodie Bouchez and Stéphane Rideau from *Les Roseaux sauvages* in a polysexual youth movie, akin to those of James Dean, in a housing

9 Téchiné wrote the preface to an edition of Nolot's *La Matiouette/La Nuit d'Ivan/ Le Café des Jules* (Nolot: 1990).
10 For more on the film, see de Baecque and Bouquet 1998, and Cravant 1998.
11 For more on this collaboration, see Frodon 1997.

estate in Villefranche-sur-Saône. *Les Chemins de l'oued* (2002) sends a young French *beur* to an Algeria consumed by conflict. The relentlessly homoerotic *Le Clan* (2004) again casts Stéphane Rideau as one of three emotionally disorientated brothers in Annecy living with their grieving (French) father and who have recently lost their (North African-born) mother. As in *Les Voleurs*, a multiple (tripartite) structure in terms of both narrative and character here rings the changes on different choices and destinies, in this case differing insertions of masculinity (married, straight/gay, factory work/alienation, violence/ renunciation) in society, and explores the relationship between childhood and adulthood, with alternating violence and lyricism.

Téchiné's other long-term collaboration has been with Martine Giordano, who worked as the editor on *La Matiouette* and who has since worked on every feature of his with the exception of *J'embrasse pas* (and *Loin*, which was shot on digital video).[12] He has tended to vary his chief cinematographers in recent years (Agnès Godard for *Les Egarés*, Hirsch for *Les Temps qui changent*), but in his earlier output he regularly used Bruno Nuytten, with whom he made four films in a row between *Souvenirs d'en France* and *Hôtel des Amériques* (Nuytten went on to direct Isabelle Adjani in *Camille Claudel*, 1988). When speaking of those 'other auteurs' (Smith 2004), the producers, the most significant in Téchiné's career have been Alain Terzian (producer of one of the very biggest French box-office hits, the time-travelling comedy *Les Visiteurs*, directed by Jean-Marie Poiré in 1993), who came to the rescue in 1985 after four years without Téchiné being able to complete a feature, thus enabling the production of *Rendez-vous*, *Le Lieu du crime* and *Les Innocents*; and Alain Sarde, whose production company has since 1974 been one of the most prolific in backing both French auteur and international independent cinema (*Mulholland Drive*, director David Lynch, 2001; *Oliver Twist*, director Roman Polanski, 2005). Sarde produced *Barocco*, was faithful to Téchiné after the failure of *Les Sœurs Brontë* (produced by Gaumont) and backed *Hôtel des Amériques*, returning for *Ma Saison préférée* (he reportedly wept when he saw the final edit) (de Baecque 1993), *Les Voleurs*, and *Alice et Martin*, since when Téchiné has had to find backing elsewhere.

12 For an interview with her, see Philippon 1988: 139-143.

Music

Téchiné was introduced to Alain Sarde by his brother Philippe, who had helped him with the scoring of *Souvenirs d'en France* by giving him musical extracts written for Pierre Granier-Deferre's *Le Train* a year before. Since then, Philippe Sarde has written the music for every Téchiné film with the exceptions of *Loin* and *Les Temps qui changent* (and also *Les Roseaux sauvages* which has no original score), and this constitutes the most extended collaboration in all of Téchiné's output. Sarde had begun writing film scores at the age of 24 for Claude Sautet's *Les Choses de la vie* (1969), and since then has been a prolific composer for French and international films, working extensively, for example, with Polanski and Tavernier. Sarde's twelve scores for Téchiné are on the whole very eclectic, and always adapted to the particular circumstances of the film. The Bernard Herrmann pastiches of *Barocco* coexist with the camp torch-song performed by Marie-France, and with the Cuban jazz motifs of Nelly/Marie-France Pisier's 'radicale' performance. In *Les Sœurs Brontë*, classical music contemporary to the period depicted is used, with developments of Beethoven, Schubert and Schumann, and the use of Rossini for Charlotte/Pisier's arrival at the opera. In the main, Sarde's music for Téchiné is consistent with the symphonic tradition of film music, with extensive use of strings, raidings of eighteenth-century music particularly Bach, open-ended pieces in the manner of Maurice Ravel, but with an ability to layer these traditions in a very plural manner, as when a baroque theme is used with contemporary harmonies in *Rendez-vous*. The score for *Les Voleurs* is his most modernist and abstract, hinting at violence, as we shall see.

Film scores, however, cannot be analysed in the same way as a discrete piece of music, since their meaning – and even their presence, the way an extract begins and ends – are dependent on the image track. Sarde intervenes in the creative process with Téchiné at a relatively late stage, when the film's editing is already well advanced. As Téchiné himself has said, the editing stage is a way of reimposing structure on the film after the shooting, which for him tends to stray from the script. So the role of Sarde's music is to establish narrative continuities, to play a role in punctuating the action, or to act as counterpoint. Needless to say, Sarde sees himself as a film composer and not a composer *tout court*, attributing this sensibility to his upbringing at the opera, where his mother was a singer:

Je pars du cinéma pour arriver à la musique, pas l'inverse ... Tout ce que j'ai vu, c'est à travers une scène, donc à travers une dramaturgie, donc à travers des personnages. Je ne conçois la musique qu'à travers ces personnages-là.[13]

However, as we might expect of as pluralist a filmmaker, Téchiné is also interested in musical digressions, 'respirations', contrasts between musical universes: 'je préfère que ça parte dans tous les sens, comme dans la vie' ('I prefer things going all over, like in real life') (Téchiné 2004). Elsewhere, Téchiné has argued in favour of the contrapuntal use of music, when it is used to introduce a feeling of strangeness in a scene that does not correspond with what is seen on the image track, most notably in music's potential for allowing the virtual to accompany the 'real': 'pour faire un peu bouger ce qui a été mis en place par l'image, et dans la conduite du récit, et pour qu'il apporte autre chose, un monde qui vient d'ailleurs, en rupture avec le naturalisme du son direct'.[14] Here Téchiné's tendency to draw on established popular music works alongside Sarde's score, and also of course with silence and the absence of music, to produce the desired effects.

As we have seen, *Les Voleurs* provides many examples of this pluralism, including Cheb Mami, Liza Minnelli, the Archies and Mozart. Sarde's score is used above all to punctuate transitions and journeys, such as the moment when Alex/Auteuil and Marie/Deneuve separate after their first conversation about Juliette, or when Marie takes Juliette to hospital. As Michel Chion puts it, music is a space–time apparatus (1985: 149). The practice of music as transition is usually embedded with other connotations. A melancholic theme on strings, developed from the very first piece of Sarde music in the diegesis, that of the boy Justin looking at his dead father, is first of all played over a shot through the hotel window of a sunlit tree blowing in the wind, and then the first scene of Alex and Juliette's lovemaking, the music then playing behind Alex's voiceover. The effect is ambiguous,

---

13 'I go from cinema to music, not the other way round ... Everything I saw was through a scene, i.e. through dramatic writing, i.e. through characters. I can conceive music only through those characters': Maillet 1985: 22.

14 'to make things move a bit in what has been put in place by the image and the conduct of the narrative, and to bring in something else, a world that comes from elsewhere, that breaks with the naturalism of direct sound', *Chants des toiles* 2001.

capable of being read, in Michel Chion's terms, as 'empathic' (accompanying a character's emotions, in this case Alex's depression and despair), 'anempathic' (contradicting the pleasure supposedly associated with sex) and also as a 'didactic counterpoint', in which the audience is invited to think about the meaning of these disjunctures, and to make links with elsewhere in the film (Chion 1985: 122–123). For example, a development from Mozart's *The Magic Flute* accompanies Alex's car journey to Marseilles, played over shots of docks and motorways, implying that Alex has internalised emotional aspects of his relationship with the now dead Marie, with whom he went to see the opera. Examples of more direct synchronisation are rare: at a moment of increasing tension and even possible danger in her relationship with Ivan, Juliette is filmed approaching his office, the rapid strings that had accompanied her renewed shoplifting now becoming more discordant; the strings that followed Marie as she took Juliette to hospital are suddenly and violently cut short when she injures her foot. Consistent with the complex narrative structure of the film, Sarde's musical motifs circulate between the fatal events of 4/5 February and periods preceding and following them, and even between the same event perceived by different protagonists, and hence by the audience at different stages of its knowledge. The shot of Juliette sitting outside the family home on the day after Ivan's death is not accompanied by music when it appears in Justin's prologue, but in Alex's narrative a closer shot of her is accompanied by the first appearance on the soundtrack of a motif on oboe that plays a key structuring element. Just as the piece featuring oboe and plucked strings was gradually replaced on the soundtrack by running water accompanying the conversation between Alex and Mireille, so is the modernist, Ravel-like piece on strings accompanying Alex and Juliette's car journey back to Lyons replaced by the sound of a screeching train, which, with its memory of the heist, may prompt Juliette's confession to Alex. This is accompanied by a theme on oboe which will now occur more frequently, with connotations of both closure and renewal, as it accompanies Alex taking the photograph of Marie asleep on his bed, his last conversation with Justin, and dominating Justin's epilogue, as it plays over his scooter ride with Jimmy and his night-time musings in bed. (Characteristically, the appearance of the final credits is contrastively accompanied by a reprise of Cheb Mami's 'Douha Alia'.)

This discussion of the collaborative dimension of Téchiné's filmmaking, and by implication that of cinema in general, is a salutary corrective to the potential pitfalls of an auteur-centred study. Nevertheless, the 'necessary fictions' involved in auteur criticism, by juxtaposing this corpus of sixteen feature films, have helped to illustrate the specificities of Téchiné's filmmaking, its unities and divergences, and also its interaction with given social, historical, industrial and aesthetic contexts. His significant place in the study of French cinema lies not only in the way he can be situated in relation to those well-established markers of the *nouvelle vague* and of May 1968, but also flags up the crucial, never to be underestimated importance for his generation of *cinéphiles* and *cinéastes*, of for example the *cinémathèque*, and of Ingmar Bergman. Téchiné is one of the key members of that generation of filmmakers which immediately followed that of the New Wave, along with Jean Eustache (b. 1938), whose output was cut short, Bertrand Blier (b. 1939), Jacques Doillon (b. 1944) and Bertrand Tavernier (b. 1941). His close association with *Cahiers du cinéma*, in the mid-1960s and the 1980s onwards, place him within a certain institutionalisation of the auteur and of course of art cinema, but this does not efface, far from it, the interaction of his work with popular forms such as the crime genre and melodrama. Téchiné continues to make films which are always relevant, always asking questions about how to live and love in this phase of capitalist modernity. (True to his tendency to make a film against the previous one, Téchiné's next project is a drama about AIDS, provisionally titled *Les Témoins*, set in Marseilles in the 1980s.) Better than most other filmmakers, he knows how to examine the relationship between the socio-historical world and what goes on inside people's heads, their desires, aspirations and potential, and hence he produces a cinema that is both emotional and intellectual. While his particular take on his south-west origins and on homosexuality contribute to his distinctiveness, these are always dynamic factors which take spectators and protagonists alike on journeys of transformation, and contribute to the production of the new. Given the urgencies generated by contemporary crises of French national self-definition, his cinema's purchase on these 'minor' and transformative modes of being acquires a particular pertinence.

References

Chants des toiles, France Musique, broadcast 16 September 2001.

Barthes, R. (1980). *La Chambre claire: note sur la photographie*. Paris, Cahiers du cinéma/Seuil.

Barthes, R. (1984). *Camera Lucida: Reflections on Photography*, translated by R. Howard. London, Fontana.

Blumenfeld, S. (1998). Gilles Taurand scénariste. *Le Monde*, 5 November, 31.

Chion M. (1985). *Le Son au cinéma*.Paris, Etoile.

Cravant, M. (1998). Note cinématographique: *L'arrière-pays* [sic] ou l'envers du bonheur. A propos d'une autre image de la campagne. *Sud-Ouest Européen*, 3, 89–92.

de Baecque, A. (1993). Journal de voix et de bruits. *Cahiers du cinéma*, 467–468 (May), 36–43.

de Baecque, A. and S. Bouquet. (1998). Jacques Nolot: le roman d'une vie. *Cahiers du cinéma*, 527 (September), 23–29.

de Baecque, A. and G. Lefort. (2004). Grâce à Téchiné, je m'envole. Il me donne la paix. Gérard Depardieu interview. *Libération*, 15 December, 2–3.

Deneuve/Téchiné, l'amour à deux. (1993). *Libération* (14 May), 32–33.

Fache, A. (2004). *Catherine Deneuve: une biographie*. Paris, Presses de la cité.

Frodon, J.-M. (1997). Christine Laurent, cinéaste: 'Filmer un combat oblige à laisser advenir les choses'. *Le Monde*, 4 September, 28.

Frodon, J.-M.(2004). Rencontre: Julien Hirsch, chef opérateur, Eloge de la méthode et de la matière, *Cahiers du cinéma*, 596 (December), 20–21.

Jameson, F. (1992). *Signatures of the Visible*. London, Routledge.

Jones, K. (1997). *André Téchiné: la estrategía de la tensión*. Valladolid, Semana internacional de cine.

Maillet, D. (1985). Philippe Sarde. *Cinématographe*, 110, 20–23.

Mérigeau, P. (2004). Rencontre avec André Téchiné. 'Je voulais réunir un couple mythique'. *Le Nouvel Observateur*, 2092 (9–15 December), 126.

Nolot, J. (1990). *La Matiouette/La Nuit d'Ivan/Le Café des Jules*. Arles, Actes Sud.

Philippon, A (1988). *André Téchiné*. Paris, Cahiers du cinéma.

Smith, A. (2004). The Other Auteurs: Producers, Cinematographers and Scriptwriters, in M. Temple and M. Witt (eds), *The French Cinema Book*. London, British Film Institute, 194–208.

Téchiné, A. (1996). Le Dépaysement humain (interview). *Nouvelle Revue Française*, 520 (May), 41–57.

Téchiné, A. (2004). CD sleeve notes. *Le Cinéma d'André Téchiné: musiques de Philippe Sarde*. Paris, Universal Music Jazz France.

Filmography

Paulina s'en va (1969) 90 min., col.

Production company: Télé Hachette Dovidis
Screenplay: André Téchiné
Photography: Jean Gonnet and William Glenn
Sound: Bernard Aubouy and René-Jean Bouyer
Editing: Fabienne Tzanck and Roland Prandini
Principal actors: Bulle Ogier (Paulina), Marie-France Pisier (Isabelle), Laura Betti (Hortense), Michèle Moretti (nurse), Yves Beneyton (Nicolas), André Julien (the old uncle), Dennis Bery (Olivier)

Souvenirs d'en France (1975) (UK/USA: French Provincial) 95 min., col.

Production company: Stephan Films, Buffalo Films, Renn Productions, Belstar Productions, Simar Films
Screenplay: André Téchiné, Marilyn Goldin
Photography: Bruno Nuytten
Sound: Pierre Befve
Music: Philippe Sarde
Editing: Anne-Marie Deshayes
Principal actors: Jeanne Moreau (Berthe), Michel Auclair (Hector), Marie-France Pisier (Régina), Claude Mann (Prosper), Orane Demazis (Augustine), Julien Guiomar (Victor), Michèle Moretti (Pierrette), Hélène Surgère (Lucie)

Barocco (1976) 105 min., col.

Production company: André Génovès, Alain Sarde
Screenplay: André Téchiné, Marilyn Goldin

Photography: Bruno Nuytten
Sound: Paul Lainé
Music: Philippe Sarde
Editing: Claudine Merlin
Principal actors: Isabelle Adjani (Laure), Gérard Depardieu (Samson), Marie-France Pisier (Nelly), Jean-Claude Brialy (Walt), Julien Guiomar (Gauthier), Hélène Surgère (Antoinette), Claude Brasseur (Nelly's husband)

Les Sœurs Brontë (1979) (USA, Australia: **The Brontë Sisters**) 115 min., col.

Production company: Action Films, Gaumont, FR3
Screenplay: Pascal Bonitzer, Jean Gruault, André Téchiné
Photography: Bruno Nuytten
Sound: Alain Curvelier
Music: Philippe Sarde
Editing: Claudine Merlin
Principal actors: Isabelle Adjani (Emily), Marie-France Pisier (Charlotte), Isabelle Huppert (Anne), Pascal Greggory (Branwell), Patrick Magee (father), Hélène Surgère (Mrs Robinson), Roland Barthes (Thackeray)

Hôtel des Amériques (1981) 93 min., col.

Production company: Alain Sarde (Sara Films), RMC, Films A2
Screenplay: Gilles Taurand, André Téchiné
Photography: Bruno Nuytten
Sound: Paul Lainé
Music: Philippe Sarde
Editing: Claudine Merlin
Principal actors: Catherine Deneuve (Hélène), Patrick Dewaere (Gilles), Etienne Chicot (Bernard), Josiane Balasko (Colette), Sabine Haudepin (Elise), François Perrot (Rudel),

La Matiouette (1983) 47 min., b/w

Production company: INA
Screenplay: Jacques Nolot, André Téchiné
Photography: Pascal Marti
Sound: Jean-Claude Brisson
Editing: Martine Giordano
Principal actors: Jacques Nolot (Alain), Patrick Fierry (Jacky)

L'Atelier (1984) 40 min., b/w and col.

Texts by: Ingmar Bergman, Pascal Bruckner, Fyodor Dostoyevsky
Production company: Nanterre-Amandiers, INA
Photography: Renato Berta
Sound: Jean-Louis Ughetto
Editing: Martine Giordano
Principal actors: Sophie Paul, Laurent Le Doyen, Marianne Chemelny, Pierre-Loup Rajot, Olivier Rabourdin, Véronique Costamagna-Prat, Christine Citti, Christophe Bernard, Claire Rigollier, Sophie Lefrou de la Colonge, Marie Carré, Nathalie Schmidt, Francis Frappat, Christine Vézinet, Nicolas Baby

Rendez-vous (1985) 87 min., col.

Production company: Alain Terzian (T. Films)
Screenplay: André Téchiné, Olivier Assayas
Photography: Renato Berta
Sound: Jean-Louis Ughetto, Dominique Hennequin
Music: Philippe Sarde
Editing: Martine Giordano
Principal actors: Juliette Binoche (Nina), Lambert Wilson (Quentin), Wadeck Stanczak (Paulot), Jean-Louis Trintignant (Scrutzler)

Le Lieu du crime (1986) (USA: **Scene of the Crime**) 90 min., col.

Production company: Alain Terzian (T. Films)
Screenplay: André Téchiné, Olivier Assayas, Pascal Bonitzer
Photography: Pascal Marti
Sound: Jean-Louis Ughetto
Music: Philippe Sarde
Editing: Martine Giordano
Principal actors: Catherine Deneuve (Lili), Victor Lanoux (Maurice), Danielle Darrieux (grandmother), Wadeck Stanczak (Martin), Nicolas Giraudi (Thomas)

Les Innocents (1987) 100 min., col.

Production company: Philippe Carcassone (Cinéa), Alain Terzian (T. Films)
Screenplay: André Téchiné, Pascal Bonitzer
Photography: Renato Berta
Sound: Jean-Louis Ughetto

Music: Philippe Sarde
Editing: Martine Giordano
Principal actors: Sandrine Bonnaire (Jeanne), Simon de la Brosse (Stéphane), Abdel Kechiche (Saïd), Jean-Claude Brialy (Klotz), Tanya Lopert (Myriam)

J'embrasse pas (1991) (USA: *I Don't Kiss*) 105 min., col.

Production company: Bac Films
Screenplay: André Téchiné, Jacques Nolot, Michel Grisolia
Photography: Thierry Arbogast
Sound: Jean-Louis Ughetto
Music: Philippe Sarde
Editing: Claudine Merlin, Edith Vassard
Principal actors: Philippe Noiret (Romain), Emmanuelle Béart (Ingrid), Manuel Blanc (Pierre), Hélène Vincent (Evelyne)

Ma Saison préférée (1993) (USA: *My Favorite Season*) 125 min., col.

Production company: Les Films Alain Sarde
Screenplay: André Téchiné, Pascal Bonitzer
Photography: Thierry Arbogast
Sound: Rémy Attal, Jean-Paul Mugel
Music: Philippe Sarde
Editing: Martine Giordano
Principal actors: Catherine Deneuve (Emilie), Daniel Auteuil (Antoine), Marthe Villalonga (Berthe), Jean-Pierre Bouvier (Bruno), Chiara Mastroianni (Anne)

Les Roseaux sauvages (1994) (USA: *Wild Reeds*) 110 min., col.

Production company: IMA, la SEPT
Screenplay: André Téchiné, Olivier Massart, Gilles Taurand
Photography: Jeanne Lapoirie
Sound: Pierre Lorrain, Jean-Paul Mugel
Editing: Martine Giordano
Principal actors: Gaël Morel (François), Elodie Bouchez (Maïté), Frédéric Gorny (Henri), Stéphane Rideau (Serge), Michèle Moretti (Mme Alvarez)

Les Voleurs (1996) (USA: Thieves) 115 min., col.

Production company: Les Films Alain Sarde
Screenplay: André Téchiné, Gilles Taurand, Michel Alexandre
Photography: Jeanne Lapoirie
Sound: Jean-Paul Mugel
Music: Philippe Sarde
Editing: Martine Giordano
Principal actors: Catherine Deneuve (Marie), Daniel Auteuil (Alex),
    Laurence Côte (Juliette), Benoît Magimel (Jimmy), Fabienne Babe
    (Mireille), Didier Bezace (Ivan)

Alice et Martin (1998) 120 min., col.

Production company: Les Films Alain Sarde, Vertigo Films
Screenplay: André Téchiné, Olivier Assayas, Gilles Taurand
Photography: Caroline Champetier
Sound: Jean-Paul Mugel
Music: Philippe Sarde
Editing: Martine Giordano
Principal actors: Juliette Binoche (Alice), Alexis Loret (Martin), Carmen
    Maura (Jeanine), Mathieu Amalric (Benjamin), Jean-Pierre Lorit
    (Frédéric), Marthe Villalonga (Lucie)

Loin (2001) 120 min., col.

Production company: UGC, Vertigo Films
Screenplay: André Téchiné, Mehdi Ben Attia, Faouzi Bensaïdi, Michel
    Alexandre
Photography: Germain Desmoulins
Sound: Joaquim Pinto
Music: Juliette Garrigues
Principal actors: Stéphane Rideau (Serge), Lubna Azabal (Sarah),
    Mohamed Hamaidi (Saïd), Yazmina Reza (Emily), Jack Taylor
    (James), Rachida Brakni (Nezha), Gaël Morel (François)

Les Egarés (2003) (USA: Strayed) 95 min., col.

Production company: FIT Productions, Spice Factory
Screenplay: André Téchiné, Gilles Taurand, based on the novella *Le
    Garçon aux yeux gris* by Gilles Perrault
Photography: Agnès Godard
Sound: Jean-Pierre Mugel

Music: Philippe Sarde

Editing: Martine Giordano

Principal actors: Emmanuelle Béart (Odile), Gaspard Ulliel (Yvan), Grégoire Leprince-Ringuet (Philippe), Clémence Meyer (Cathy), Samuel Labarthe (Robert), Jean Fornerod (Georges)

Les Temps qui changent (2004) 90 min., col.

Production company: Gémini Films

Screenplay: André Téchiné, Pascal Bonitzer, Laurent Guyot

Photography: Julien Hirsch

Sound: Jean-Paul Mugel, Francis Wargnier

Music: Juliette Garrigues

Editing: Martine Giordano

Principal actors: Catherine Deneuve (Cécile), Gérard Depardieu (Antoine), Gilbert Melki (Natan), Malik Zidi (Sami), Lubna Azabal (Nadia/Aïcha), Tanya Lopert (Rachel), Nadem Rachati (Bilal)

Select bibliography

Books on Téchiné

Jones, K. (1997). *André Téchiné: la estrategía de la tensión*, translated by Carlos Herrero, Valladolid, Festival internacional de cine. The New York-based film critic Kent Jones, who co-wrote with Martin Scorsese the script for his analysis of Italian cinema, *Mio Viaggio in Italia* (1999), has produced a book on Téchiné which is currently available only in Spanish, as it accompanied the Valladolid Film Festival's Téchiné retrospective. After an introductory essay which is strong on aspects of Téchiné's cinema such as movement, childhood and modernity, the book goes through fourteen films in turn, up to and including *Les Voleurs*, although Jones has not seen *Paulina s'en va*. Interviews follow with Téchiné and with Olivier Assayas. For non-readers of Spanish, a much shorter version of Jones' appreciative and sensitive comments on Téchiné's cinema can be found in his article: (1996). People are the Opposite of Silence. *Metro Magazine*, 107, 3–9.

Philippon, A. (1988). *André Téchiné*, Paris, Cahiers du cinéma. This is still the only full-length study in French on Téchiné. Philippon (who died in 1998) provides interesting analyses, often influenced by psychoanalysis, of the films, but this study stops at *Les Innocents*, and so covers only half of the feature-film output. The book does a thorough job on Téchiné's emergence as a filmmaker, and in the appendix there are useful interviews with Pascal Bonitzer, Renato Berta, Martine Giordano and Téchiné himself.

Other articles and chapters on Téchiné

The most sustained discussion of Téchiné available in English is that of Jill Forbes, who devotes half of the final chapter, 'The New History Film', of her *The Cinema in France After the New Wave* (London: BFI/Macmillan, 1992) to a discussion of Téchiné's output from *Souvenirs d'en France* to *Les Innocents*. Investigating his treatment of 'the petty bourgeois consciousness' and 'the exploration of spectacle' she concludes that in his films 'the opposition between naturalism and aestheticism has been rendered obsolete' (p. 258).

Les Roseaux sauvages is the film which has drawn the most attention from academics writing in English, being examined in:

Everett, W. (1999). Films at the Crossroads: *Les Roseaux sauvages* (Téchiné, 1994), in P. Powrie (ed.), *French Cinema in the 1990s: Continuity and Difference*. Oxford University Press, 141–152.

Rollet, B. (2002). Remembering the Algerian War: Memory/ies and Identity/ies in Téchiné's *Les Roseaux Sauvages*, in M. S. Alexander, M. Evans and J. F. V. Keiger (eds), *The Algerian War and the French Army, 1954–1962: Experiences, Images, Testimonies*. London, Palgrave, 200–210.

Wilson, E. (1999). *French Cinema since 1950: Personal Histories*. London, Duckworth.

A discussion of *Les Roseaux sauvages* and its relation to previous Téchiné films is to be found in: White, A. (1995). Strange Gifts: André Téchiné Remakes the Melodrama. *Film Comment*, 31 (July), 70–75.

One of the few articles in French to home in on Téchiné's treatment of masculinity and homosexuality is: Brassart, A. (2000). Une Critique du modèle masculin: à propos des films d'André Téchiné, in D. Welzer-Lang (ed), *Nouvelles approches des hommes et du masculin*. Toulouse, Presses universitaires du Mirail, 313–319.

Index

Note: 'n.' after a page reference indicates the number of a note on that page